"InterVarsity Press is doing a ve _____ g _____
The Contemporary Christian back into print—slightly modernized,
helpfully rearranged, and broken into short, reader-friendly books.
The result is a boon to a new generation of readers who will greatly
benefit, as many have before, from Stott's thorough grounding in
Scripture, unusual help for living the Christian life, and perceptive
interaction with the contemporary world."

Mark Noll, author of *The Rise of Evangelicalism*

"I have long benefited from the work of John Stott because of the way
he combines rigorous engagement of the biblical text and careful
engagement with the culture of his day. The God's Word for Today
series presents Stott at his very best. This series displays his
commitment to biblical authority, his zeal for the mission of the
church, and his call to faithful witness in the world. Stott's reflections
here are a must-read for church leaders today."

Trevin Wax, director of Bibles and reference at LifeWay Christian
Resources, author of *This Is Our Time* and *Eschatological Discipleship*

"Imagine being a child overwhelmed by hundreds of jigsaw puzzle
pieces—you just can't put them together! And then imagine a kindly
old uncle comes along and helps you put the whole thing together
piece by piece. That is what it felt like reading John Stott's *The
Contemporary Christian.* For those of us who feel we can't get our head
around our Bible, let alone our world, he comes along and, with his
staggering gifts of clarity and insight, helps us step by step to work out
what it means to understand our world through biblical lenses. It's
then a great blessing to have Tim Chester's questions at the end of each
chapter, which help us think through and internalize each step."

Rico Tice, senior minister for evangelism, All Souls Langham Place,
London, coauthor of *Christianity Explored*

"Vintage Stott, with all that that implies. In it, as usual, we find him digesting and deploying a wide range of material with a symmetry matching that of Mozart, a didactic force like that of J. C. Ryle, and a down-to-earth common sense that reminds us of G. K. Chesterton. It is really a pastoral essay, a sermon on paper aimed at changing people . . . an outstandingly good book."

J. I. Packer, in *Christianity Today*

"In my formative years as a young Christian, I was acutely aware of the fact that I faced many challenges to Christian thinking and behavior. Few writers helped me understand how I should respond to these challenges and think and live as a Christian as much as John Stott did. The challenges of faithfulness to God's way are more acute and complex today than when I was a young Christian. In these little books you find the essence of Stott's thinking about the Christian life, and it is refreshing to read again and see how relevant and health giving this material is for today. I'm grateful to InterVarsity Press and to Tim Chester for making Stott's thinking accessible to a new generation."

Ajith Fernando, teaching director, Youth for Christ, Sri Lanka

"It is always refreshing, enlightening, and challenging reading from the pen of John Stott. I am totally delighted that one of his most significant works will continue to be available, hopefully for more decades to come. The way Stott strives to be faithful to the Word of God and relevant to his world—secularized Western society—as the locus for the drama of God's action is exemplary, especially for those of us ordained to the service of the church in our diverse contexts. I highly commend the God's Word for Today series to all who share the same pursuit—listening intently to God's Word and God's world, hearing and obeying God."

David Zac Niringiye, author of *The Church: God's Pilgrim People*

"I am delighted that a new generation will now be able to benefit from this rich teaching, which so helped me when it first appeared. As always with John Stott, there is a wonderful blend of faithful exposition of the Bible, rigorous engagement with the world, and challenging applications for our lives."

Vaughan Roberts, author of *God's Big Picture*

"Technology has enabled more voices to clamor for our attention than ever before; while at the same time, people's ability to listen carefully seems to have deteriorated like never before. John Stott's speaking and writing was renowned for two things in particular. He taught us how to listen attentively to God in order to live faithfully for God, and he too modeled how to listen to the world sensitively in order to communicate God's purposes intelligibly. He taught us to listen. That is why it is such a thrill to see *The Contemporary Christian* carefully revived in a new format as this series for a new generation of readers. As we read, may we listen well!"

Mark Meynell, director (Europe and Caribbean) of Langham Preaching, Langham Partnership, author of *When Darkness Seems My Closest Friend*

with
TIM CHESTER

John Stott

The Bible

GOD'S WORD FOR TODAY

An imprint of InterVarsity Press
Downers Grove, Illinois

InterVarsity Press, USA
P.O. Box 1400
Downers Grove, IL 60515-1426, USA
ivpress.com
email@ivpress.com

Inter-Varsity Press, England
36 Causton Street
London SW1P 4ST, England
ivpbooks.com
ivp@ivpbooks.com

This volume has been adapted from John Stott, The Contemporary Christian (1992), and is one of five titles published in this format in the God's Word for Today series, with extra text, including questions, by Tim Chester. Published by Inter-Varsity Press, England, as The Contemporary Christian series.

InterVarsity Press®, USA, is the book-publishing division of InterVarsity Christian Fellowship/USA® and a member movement of the International Fellowship of Evangelical Students. Website: intervarsity.org.

Inter-Varsity Press, England, originated within the Inter-Varsity Fellowship, now the Universities and Colleges Christian Fellowship, a student movement connecting Christian Unions in universities and colleges throughout Great Britain, and a member movement of the International Fellowship of Evangelical Students. Website: uccf.org.uk.

Cover design: Mark Read
Image: Kumiko Shimizu/Unsplash

USA ISBN 978-0-8308-4368-8 (print)
USA ISBN 978-0-8308-6448-5 (digital)
UK ISBN 978-1-78359-770-3 (print)
UK ISBN 978-1-78359-771-0 (digital)

Typeset in Great Britain by CRB Associates, Potterhanworth, Lincolnshire
Printed in the United States of America ♾

InterVarsity Press is committed to ecological stewardship and to the conservation of natural resources in all our operations. This book was printed using sustainably sourced paper.

Library of Congress Cataloging-in-Publication Data

A catalog record for this book is available from the Library of Congress.

P	22	21	20	19	18	17	16	15	14	13	12	11	10	9	8	7	6	5	4	3	2	1
Y	39	38	37	36	35	34	33	32	31	30	29	28	27	26	25	24	23	22	21	20	19

Contents

About the authors

John Stott had a worldwide ministry as a church leader, a Bible expositor and the author of many award-winning books. He was Rector Emeritus of All Souls, Langham Place, London, and Founder-President of the Langham Partnership.

Tim Chester is Pastor of Grace Church, Boroughbridge, North Yorkshire, Chair of Keswick Ministries and the author of more than forty books.

Preface

To be 'contemporary' is to live in the present, and to move with the times without worrying too much about the past or the future.

To be a 'contemporary Christian', however, is to live in a present which is enriched by our knowledge of the past and by our expectation of the future. Our Christian faith demands this. Why? Because the God we trust and worship is 'the Alpha and the Omega . . . who is, and who was, and who is to come, the Almighty',[1] while the Jesus Christ we follow is 'the same yesterday and today and for ever'.[2]

So this book and series are about how Christians handle time – how we can bring the past, the present and the future together in our thinking and living. Two main challenges face us. The first is the tension between the 'then' (past) and the 'now' (present), and the second the tension between the 'now' (present) and the 'not yet' (future).

The Introduction opens up the first problem. Is it possible for us truly to honour the past and live in the present at the same time? Can we preserve Christianity's historic identity intact without cutting ourselves off from those around us? Can we communicate the gospel in ways that are exciting and modern without distorting or even destroying it? Can we be authentic and fresh at the same time, or do we have to choose?

The Conclusion opens up the second problem: the tension between the 'now' and the 'not yet'. How far can we explore and experience everything that God has said and done through Christ without straying into what has not yet been revealed or given? How can we develop a proper sense of humility about a future yet to unfold without becoming complacent about where we are in the present?

In between these enquiries into the influences of the past and the future comes an exploration about our Christian responsibilities in the present.

Preface

This series is about questions of doctrine and discipleship under the five headings: 'The Gospel', 'The Disciple', 'The Bible' (the book you are holding in your hands), 'The Church' and 'The World', though I make no attempt to be systematic, let alone exhaustive.

In addition to the topic of time, and the relations between past, present and future, there is a second theme running through this series: the need for us to talk less and listen more.

I believe we are called to the difficult and even painful task of 'double listening'. We are to listen carefully (although of course with differing degrees of respect) both to the ancient Word and to the modern world, in order to relate the one to the other with a combination of faithfulness and sensitivity.

Each book in this series is an attempt at double listening. It is my firm conviction that if we can only develop our capacity for double listening, we will avoid the opposite pitfalls of unfaithfulness and irrelevance, and truly be able to speak God's Word to God's world with effectiveness today.

Adapted from the original Preface by John Stott in 1991

A note to the reader

The original book entitled *The Contemporary Christian*, on which this volume and series are based, may not seem 'contemporary' to readers more than a quarter of a century later. But both the publisher and John Stott's Literary Executors are convinced that the issues which John Stott addresses in this book are every bit as relevant today as when they were first written.

The question was how to make this seminal work accessible for new generations of readers. We have sought to do this in the following ways:

- The original work has been divided into a series of several smaller volumes based on the five major sections of the original.
- Words that may not resonate with the twenty-first-century reader have been updated, while great care has been taken to maintain the thought process and style of the author in the original.
- Each chapter is now followed by questions from a current bestselling Christian author to aid reflection and response.

Lovers of the original work have expressed delight that this book is being made available in a way that extends its reach and influence well into a new century. We pray that your life will be enriched as you read, as the lives of many have already been greatly enriched by the original edition.

Series introduction
The Contemporary Christian:
the then and the now

The expression 'the contemporary Christian' strikes many as a contradiction in terms. Isn't Christianity an antique relic from the remote past, irrelevant to people in today's world?

My purpose in this series is to show that there is such a thing as 'contemporary Christianity' – not something newfangled, but original, historic, orthodox, biblical Christianity, sensitively related to the modern world.

Christianity: both historical and contemporary

We begin by reaffirming that Christianity is a historical religion. Of course, every religion arose in a particular historical context. Christianity, however, makes an especially strong claim to be historical because it rests not only on a historical *person*, Jesus of Nazareth, but on certain historical *events* which involved him, especially his birth, death and resurrection. There is a common thread here with the Judaism from which Christianity sprang. The Old Testament presents God not only as 'the God of Abraham, Isaac and Jacob', but also as the God of the covenant which he made with Abraham, and then renewed with Isaac and Jacob. Again, he is not only 'the God of Moses', but is also seen as the Redeemer responsible for the exodus, who went on to renew the covenant yet again at Mount Sinai.

Christians are forever tethered in heart and mind to these decisive, historical events of the past. We are constantly encouraged in the

Bible to look back to them with thankfulness. Indeed, God deliberately made provision for his people to recall his saving actions on a
regular basis. Supremely, the Lord's Supper or Holy Communion
enables us to call the atoning death of Christ regularly to mind, and
so bring the past into the present.

But the problem is that Christianity's foundational events took
place such a long time ago. I had a conversation with two brothers
some years ago – students who told me they had turned away from
the faith of their parents. One was now an agnostic, the other an
atheist. I asked why. Did they no longer believe in the truth of
Christianity? No, their dilemma was not whether Christianity was
true, but whether it was *relevant*. How could it be? Christianity, they
went on, was a primitive, Palestinian religion from long ago. So what
on earth did it have to offer them, living in the exciting modern
world?

This view of Christianity is widespread. The world has changed
dramatically since Jesus' day, and goes on changing with ever
more bewildering speed. People reject the gospel, not necessarily
because they think it false, but because it no longer resonates with
them.

In response to this we need to be clear about the basic Christian
conviction that God continues to speak through what he has spoken.
His Word is not a prehistoric fossil, but a living message for the contemporary world. Even granted the historical particularities of the
Bible and the immense complexities of the modern world, there is
still a fundamental correspondence between them. God's Word
remains a lamp to our feet and a light for our path.[1]

At the same time, our dilemma remains. Can Christianity both
retain its authentic identity *and* demonstrate its relevance?

The desire to present Jesus in a way that appeals to our own generation is obviously right. This was the preoccupation of the German
pastor Dietrich Bonhoeffer while in prison during World War 2:
'What is bothering me incessantly,' he wrote, 'is the question . . . who

2

Christ really is for us today?'[2] It is a difficult question. In answering it, the church has tended in every generation to develop images of Christ which deviate from the portrait painted by the New Testament authors.

Attempting to modernize Jesus

Here are some of the church's many attempts to present a contemporary picture of Christ, some of which have been more successful than others in remaining loyal to the original.

I think first of *Jesus the ascetic* who inspired generations of monks and hermits. He was much like John the Baptist, for he too dressed in a camel's hair cloak, wore sandals or went barefoot, and munched locusts with evident relish. But it would be hard to reconcile this portrait with his contemporaries' criticism that he was a party-goer who 'came eating and drinking'.[3]

Then there was *Jesus the pale Galilean*. The apostate emperor Julian tried to reinstate Rome's pagan gods after Constantine had replaced them with the worship of Christ, and is reported as having said on his deathbed in AD 363, 'You have conquered, O Galilean.' His words were popularized by the nineteenth-century poet Swinburne:

Thou hast conquered, O pale Galilean;
The world has grown grey from thy breath.

This image of Jesus was perpetuated in medieval art and stained glass, with a heavenly halo and a colourless complexion, eyes lifted to the sky and feet never quite touching the ground.

In contrast to the presentations of Jesus as weak, suffering and defeated, there was *Jesus the cosmic Christ*, much loved by the Byzantine church leaders. They depicted him as the King of kings and Lord of lords, the creator and ruler of the universe. Yet, exalted high above all things, glorified and reigning, he seemed aloof from

3

the real world, and even from his own humanity, as revealed in the incarnation and the cross.

At the opposite end of the theological spectrum, the seventeenth- and eighteenth-century deists of the Enlightenment constructed in their own image *Jesus the teacher of common sense*,[4] entirely human and not divine at all. The most dramatic example is the work of Thomas Jefferson, President of the United States from 1801 to 1809. Rejecting the supernatural as incompatible with reason, he produced his own edition of the Gospels, in which all miracles and mysteries were systematically eliminated. What is left is a guide to a merely human moral teacher.

In the twentieth century we were presented with a wide range of options. Two of the best known owe their popularity to musicals. There is *Jesus the clown* of *Godspell*, who spends his time singing and dancing, and thus captures something of the gaiety of Jesus, but hardly takes his mission seriously. Somewhat similar is *Jesus Christ Superstar* the disillusioned celebrity, who once thought he knew who he was, but in Gethsemane was no longer sure.

The late President of Cuba, Fidel Castro, frequently referred to Jesus as 'a great revolutionary', and there have been many attempts to portray him as *Jesus the freedom fighter*, the urban guerrilla, the first-century Che Guevara, with black beard and flashing eyes, whose most characteristic gesture was to overthrow the tables of the moneychangers and to drive them out of the temple with a whip.

These different portraits illustrate the recurring tendency to update Christ in line with current fashions. It began in the apostolic age, with Paul needing to warn of false teachers who were preaching 'a Jesus other than the Jesus we [apostles] preached'.[5] Each succeeding generation tends to read back into him its own ideas and hopes, and create him in its own image.

Their motive is right (to paint a contemporary portrait of Jesus), but the result is always distorted (as the portrait is unauthentic). The challenge before us is to present Jesus to our generation in ways that are both accurate and appealing.

Calling for double listening

The main reason for every betrayal of the authentic Jesus is that we pay too much attention to contemporary trends and too little to God's Word. The thirst for relevance becomes so demanding that we feel we have to give in to it, whatever the cost. We become slaves to the latest fad, prepared to sacrifice truth on the altar of modernity. The quest for relevance degenerates into a lust for popularity. For the opposite extreme to irrelevance is accommodation, a feeble-minded, unprincipled surrender to the spirit of the time.

God's people live in a world which can be actively hostile. We are constantly exposed to the pressure to conform.

Thank God, however, that there have always been those who have stood firm, sometimes alone, and refused to compromise. I think of Jeremiah in the sixth century BC, and Paul in his day ('everyone . . . has deserted me'),[6] Athanasius in the fourth century and Luther in the sixteenth.

In our own day we too need to resolve to present the biblical gospel in such a way as to speak to modern dilemmas, fears and frustrations, but with equal determination not to compromise it in so doing. Some stumbling-blocks are intrinsic to the original gospel and cannot be eliminated or soft-pedalled in order to make it easier to accept. The gospel contains some features so alien to modern thought that it will always appear foolish, however hard we strive to show that it is 'true and reasonable'.[7] The cross will always be an assault on human self-righteousness and a challenge to human self-indulgence. Its 'scandal' (stumbling-block) simply cannot be removed. The church speaks most authentically not when it has become indistinguishable from the world around us, but when its distinctive light shines most brightly.

However keen we are to communicate God's Word to others, we must be faithful to that Word and, if necessary, be prepared to suffer for it. God's word to Ezekiel encourages us: 'Do not be afraid of them . . . You must speak my words to them, whether they listen or fail to listen, for they are rebellious.'[8] Our calling is to be faithful and relevant, not merely trendy.

How then can we develop a Christian mind which is both shaped by the truths of historic, biblical Christianity and also fully immersed in the realities of the contemporary world? We have to begin with a double refusal. We refuse to become either so absorbed in the Word that we *escape* into it and fail to let it confront the world, or so absorbed in the world that we *conform* to it and fail to subject it to the judgment of the Word.

In place of this double refusal, we are called to double listening. We need to listen to the Word of God with expectancy and humility, ready for God perhaps to confront us with a word that may be disturbing and uninvited. And we must also listen to the world around us. The voices we hear may take the form of shrill and strident protest. There will also be the anguished cries of those who are suffering, and the pain, doubt, anger, alienation and even despair of those who are at odds with God. We listen to the Word with humble reverence, anxious to understand it, and resolved to believe and obey what we come to understand. We listen to the world with critical alertness, anxious to understand it too, and resolved not necessarily to believe and obey it, but to sympathize with it and to seek grace to discover how the gospel relates to it.

Everybody finds listening difficult. But are Christians sometimes less good at listening than others? We can learn from the so-called 'comforters' in the Old Testament book of Job. They began well. When they heard about Job's troubles, they came to visit him and, seeing how great his sufferings were, said nothing to him for a whole week. If only they had continued as they began, and kept their mouths shut! Instead, they trotted out their conventional view – that every sinner suffers for his or her own sins – in the most insensitive way. They did not really listen to what Job had to say. They merely repeated their own thoughtless and heartless claptrap, until in the end God stepped in and rebuked them for having misrepresented him.

We need to cultivate 'double listening', the ability to listen to two voices at the same time – the voice of God through the Bible and the voices of men and women around us. These voices will often contradict one another, but our purpose in listening to them both is to discover how they relate to each other. Double listening is indispensable to Christian discipleship and to Christian mission.

It is only through this discipline of double listening that it is possible to become a 'contemporary Christian'. We bring 'historical' and 'contemporary' together as we learn to apply the Word to the world, proclaiming good news which is both true and new.

To put it in a nutshell, we live in the 'now' in the light of the 'then'.

The Bible
Introduction

'We present you with this Book, the most valuable thing that this world affords. Here is wisdom; this is the royal law; these are the lively oracles of God.' With these words in the coronation service the Moderator of the General Assembly of the Church of Scotland handed Queen Elizabeth a copy of the Bible when she was crowned in 1953.

It might be tempting to dismiss such claims for the Bible as idle rhetoric, were it not that successive generations of Christian people have found them to be true. Scripture has brought us light in darkness, strength in weakness, comfort in sadness. And so we readily endorse the psalmist's declaration that the words of God 'are more precious than gold, than much pure gold; they are sweeter than honey, than honey from the comb'.[1]

So it has been distressing in the West to watch the Bible being dislodged from its position of acknowledged authority, not only in the nation but also in the church. There is little hope for thoroughgoing national reform or church renewal unless the Word of God is once more widely respected, and its teaching followed.

This book is my small contribution to this goal, as I write about the urgent need to continue in, respond to, interpret and expound God's Word.

1

Continuing in the Word

It is a regular theme of the New Testament authors that the people of God must be steadfast. On the one hand, we must resist the intellectual and moral pressures of our contemporary world, and refuse to conform to the trends and fashions of the day. We are not to let ourselves slip, slither and slide in the mud of relativity. We cannot let ourselves be torn from our moorings and be carried away by the flood. On the other hand, we are positively called to persevere in the truth we have received, to cling to it as a secure handhold in the storm, and to stand firm on this foundation.

Here are some examples of this kind of exhortation, by three of the major contributors to the New Testament.

Paul: 'So then, brothers and sisters, stand firm and hold fast to the teachings we passed on to you.'[1]

Hebrews: 'We must pay the most careful attention, therefore, to what we have heard, so that we do not drift away.'[2]

John: 'See that what you have heard from the beginning remains in you.'[3] 'Anyone who runs ahead and does not continue in the teaching of Christ does not have God; whoever continues in the teaching has both the Father and the Son.'[4]

Common to these quotations is the recognition that certain truths had been 'taught' or 'passed on' by the apostles, and had consequently been 'heard' or 'received' by the church. This body of doctrine was now a sacred deposit to be guarded.[5] It had a normative quality. The church must remain in it and hold to it, neither going back from it, nor going on beyond it in such a way as to contradict it.

Part of Paul's final charge to Timothy elaborates this theme. In order to grasp its implications, we need to have 2 Timothy 3:1 – 4:8 before us.

3 ¹But mark this: there will be terrible times in the last days. ²People will be lovers of themselves, lovers of money, boastful, proud, abusive, disobedient to their parents, ungrateful, unholy, ³without love, unforgiving, slanderous, without self-control, brutal, not lovers of the good, ⁴treacherous, rash, conceited, lovers of pleasure rather than lovers of God – ⁵having a form of godliness but denying its power. Have nothing to do with such people.

⁶They are the kind who worm their way into homes and gain control over gullible women, who are loaded down with sins and are swayed by all kinds of evil desires, ⁷always learning but never able to come to a knowledge of the truth. ⁸Just as Jannes and Jambres opposed Moses, so also these teachers oppose the truth. They are men of depraved minds, who, as far as the faith is concerned, are rejected. ⁹But they will not get very far because, as in the case of those men, their folly will be clear to everyone.

¹⁰You, however, know all about my teaching, my way of life, my purpose, faith, patience, love, endurance, ¹¹persecutions, sufferings – what kinds of things happened to me in Antioch, Iconium and Lystra, the persecutions I endured. Yet the Lord rescued me from all of them. ¹²In fact, everyone who wants to live a godly life in Christ Jesus will be persecuted, ¹³while evildoers and impostors will go from bad to worse, deceiving and being deceived. ¹⁴But as for you, continue in what you have learned and have become convinced of, because you know those from whom you learned it, ¹⁵and how from infancy you have known the Holy Scriptures, which are able to make you wise for salvation through faith in Christ Jesus. ¹⁶All

Scripture is God-breathed and is useful for teaching, rebuking, correcting and training in righteousness, [17] so that the servant of God may be thoroughly equipped for every good work.

4 [1] In the presence of God and of Christ Jesus, who will judge the living and the dead, and in view of his appearing and his kingdom, I give you this charge: [2] preach the word; be prepared in season and out of season; correct, rebuke and encourage – with great patience and careful instruction. [3] For the time will come when people will not put up with sound doctrine. Instead, to suit their own desires, they will gather round them a great number of teachers to say what their itching ears want to hear. [4] They will turn their ears away from the truth and turn aside to myths. [5] But you, keep your head in all situations, endure hardship, do the work of an evangelist, discharge all the duties of your ministry.

[6] For I am already being poured out like a drink offering, and the time for my departure is near. [7] I have fought the good fight, I have finished the race, I have kept the faith. [8] Now there is in store for me the crown of righteousness, which the Lord, the righteous Judge, will award to me on that day – and not only to me, but also to all who have longed for his appearing.

Standing in the Word

Paul's exhortation to Timothy was given against the background of the kind of society he was living in (3:1–13). It was a context that was hostile to the gospel. Nor could the gospel be reshaped in order to accommodate to society's ideas and standards. On the contrary, Paul was aware of a radical incompatibility between the Word and the world. 'Mark this,' he wrote: 'There will be terrible times in the last days.'

It is important to realize that by 'the last days' the apostle was not alluding to some future era immediately preceding the return of

Christ. For in verse 5 he tells Timothy to 'have nothing to do' with the people he has been describing. How could Timothy avoid them if they had not yet been born? No, 'the last days' from the perspective of the New Testament began with Jesus Christ. He ushered them in.[6] The last days are therefore these days, the days in which Timothy lived and in which we also live. They are the whole period between the first and second comings of Christ.

What are the characteristics of the last days? Three seem to stand out from Paul's description.

The first is *misdirected love*. Of the nineteen distinguishing marks which the apostle lists (verses 2–4), it is striking that six have to do with love. 'People will be lovers of themselves, lovers of money . . . without love . . . not lovers of the good . . . lovers of pleasure rather than lovers of God.' The expression 'without love' must be understood as meaning 'without true love'. For the people in view are not devoid of love altogether; they love themselves, they love money and they love pleasure. But these are examples of *misdirected* love. Self, money and pleasure are inappropriate objects of human love. They even become idolatrous when they displace God from his rightful place as the One to be loved with all our being. Yet we see misdirected love everywhere today. Self-absorption, covetousness and hedonism are rife, while the first and second commandments, to love God and our neighbour, are neglected. Moreover, when people's love is directed to the wrong objects, all their relationships go wrong. They become 'boastful, proud, abusive, disobedient . . . ungrateful . . . unforgiving, slanderous' (verses 2–3).

The second characteristic of our age is *empty religion*. Our contemporaries are described as 'having a form of godliness but denying its power' (verse 5). It may seem extraordinary that people characterized by self-love could also be religious. But this is what Paul says. Indeed, it is possible for religion, which is intended to express the worship of God, to become perverted into a means of ego-inflation. The proper name for this sick distortion is hypocrisy, and Jesus vehemently attacked it.[7] Such religion is 'form' without 'power', outward show without inward reality. It is also an enemy of the gospel, because nominal Christianity hardens people against real Christianity.

Third, the last days are distinguished by *the cult of an open mind.* Paul writes here of people who are 'always learning but never able to come to a knowledge of the truth' (verse 7). They sit on the fence and refuse to come down on either side of it. Tolerance is their watchword. Determined to avoid the pain of reaching definite conclusions, they make a fetish of keeping their mind open. They cannot endure what C. S. Lewis called 'the tyrannous noon of revelation';[8] they prefer the twilight of free thought. They have overlooked the distinction which Allan Bloom pointed out between two kinds of 'openness' – 'the openness of indifference . . . and the openness that invites us to the quest for knowledge and certitude'.[9] The latter is an aspect of the Christian virtue of humility, acknowledging that our understanding is provisional and incomplete, and always seeking to increase it. The former, on the other hand, is not only insulting to truth, but personally perilous. It exposes us to the danger, as one bishop has put it, of having our minds so open that our brains fall out!

Here, then, are three characteristics of our time, which Scripture resolutely criticizes and tells us to avoid.

- We are to love God and our neighbour, and not misdirect our love to self, money or pleasure.
- We are to value the reality and power of religion above its outward forms.
- We are to submit humbly to God's revelation and not cultivate a wishy-washy undemanding agnosticism.

Thus, Paul calls Timothy to be different from the world around him. After his portrayal of these ungodly trends, Paul twice writes *su de,* which is translated 'You, however', and then 'But as for you' in verses

10 and 14. These words introduce the apostle's two exhortations to Timothy to resist the mood of the world. The first exhortation focuses on what Timothy has already come to know about Paul: his 'teaching', his 'way of life', his 'purpose', together with his 'faith, patience, love, endurance, persecutions, sufferings' (verses 10–13). Timothy had seen Paul's ministry with his own eyes, including the opposition and persecution which he had had to endure in Antioch, Iconium and Lystra (verse 11). For the fact is that 'everyone who wants to live a godly life in Christ Jesus will be persecuted' (verse 12), since 'evildoers and impostors', who reject the gospel, 'will go from bad to worse' (verse 13).

Thus, the apostle contrasts the low standards of the world with his own teaching and conduct. The two were in irreconcilable antagonism to one another. Hence the persecution Paul had had to bear. If Timothy were to stand firm, taking Paul's side against the world's, he would undoubtedly have to suffer too.

Continuing in the Word

Paul's mention of the 'evildoers and impostors', deceiving and being deceived, who would 'go from bad to worse' (verse 13), leads him to his second *su de*, 'But as for you'. This time, rather than just looking back to his past teaching, conduct and sufferings which Timothy had come to know, he also looks to the future: 'But as for you, continue in what you have learned and have become convinced of, because you know those from whom you learned it' (verse 14). These teachers from whom Timothy had learned are probably first his mother and grandmother who had taught him the Old Testament from his infancy (verse 15; cf. 1:5), and second the apostle, whose 'teaching' (verse 10) Timothy knew and which for us is preserved in the New Testament. Thus, Paul contrasts two sets of teachers – on the one hand, the impostors and deceivers of verse 13, and on the other, Timothy's mother and mentor (the apostle himself) who had taught him the Scriptures.

Today we too need to pay attention to the same summons. We are not to be like reeds blown by the wind. We are not to bow down before the prevailing trends of society, with its covetousness and materialism, its relativism, and its rejection of all absolute standards of truth and goodness. Instead, we are to continue faithfully in the Old and New Testament Scriptures.

But why? What is Scripture that it should occupy such an important place in our lives? The apostle goes on to stress three fundamental aspects of it.

First, *Scripture is able to instruct us for salvation* (verse 15, RSV). Its primary purpose is practical. It is more a guidebook than a textbook, more a book of salvation than a book of science. This is not to say that the biblical and scientific accounts of the world are in conflict, but rather that they are complementary. God's purpose in Scripture is not to reveal facts that can be discovered by the scientific method of observation and experiment, but rather to reveal truths which are beyond the scope of science, in particular God's way of salvation through Christ.

This is why Jesus Christ is himself the centre of the biblical revelation, since it bears witness to him.[10] As J.-J. von Allmen has expressed it, 'the heart of the Scripture (what sums it up and makes it live) or the head of the Scripture (. . . what explains it and justifies it) . . . is Jesus Christ. To read the Bible without meeting him is to read it badly, and to preach the Bible without proclaiming him is to preach it falsely.'[11] It is because Scripture instructs us for salvation that it instructs us about Christ, by faith in whom we receive salvation. Moreover, the reason we love the Bible is that it speaks to us of Christ. It is God's picture, God's portrait, of Christ.

Second, *Scripture is God-breathed.* The better-known AV phrase consists of five words, 'given by inspiration of God'. But the NIV is correct to use the one word 'God-breathed' as the precise equivalent of the Greek expression *theopneustos.* This tells us that Scripture is the Word of God, spoken by God, or breathed out of the mouth of

God. The implied combination of mouth, breath and word shows that the model of inspiration which is intended is that of human speech. For speech is communication between minds. Often we keep what is 'on our mind' to ourselves. But when we speak, we clothe the thoughts of our minds in the words of our mouth.

We observe also that the text reads, 'All Scripture is God-breathed' (verse 16). The NEB, on the other hand, translates the clause 'every inspired Scripture is useful'. This is almost certainly incorrect. It implies that if every inspired Scripture is useful, there must be other Scriptures which are not inspired and therefore not useful. But, in the first place, the concept of 'uninspired Scripture' is a contradiction in terms since the word 'Scripture' simply means inspired writing. Second, the NEB omits, without sufficient warrant, the little word *kai*, meaning 'and' or 'also'. It shows that Paul is not making one statement ('every inspired Scripture is useful'), but two ('every Scripture is inspired *and* useful'). Indeed, it is useful to us precisely because it is inspired by God.

Nevertheless, we must not mis-state the truth of inspiration. When God spoke, he did not speak into space. Nor did he write documents and leave them around to be discovered, as Joseph Smith (founder of the Mormon Church) claimed regarding his golden plates. Nor did God dictate Scripture to non-participating secretaries, as Muslims believe Allah dictated the Qur'an to Muhammad in Arabic. No, by the process of inspiration we mean that the human authors, even while God was speaking to and through them, were themselves actively engaged in historical research, theological reflection and literary composition. For much of Scripture is historical narrative, and each author has his own particular theological emphasis and literary style. Divine inspiration did not dispense with human co-operation, or iron out the peculiar contributions of the authors.

So 'God-breathed' is not the only account which Scripture gives of itself, since God's mouth was not the only mouth involved in its production. The same Scripture which says 'the mouth of the LORD has spoken'[12] also says that God spoke 'by the mouth of his holy prophets'.[13] Out of whose mouth did Scripture come then? God's or the prophet's? The only biblical answer is 'both'. Indeed, God spoke through the human authors in such a way that his words were simultaneously their words, and their words were simultaneously his. This is the double authorship of the Bible. Scripture is equally the Word of God and the words of human beings. Even better, it is the Word of God through the words of human beings.

It is essential to keep the two authorships together. Some theologians, ancient and modern, Catholic and Protestant, have appealed to the two natures of Christ as an analogy. Although the parallel is not exact, it is illuminating. In the person of Christ (who is both God and human) we must neither affirm his deity in such a way as to deny his humanity, nor affirm his humanity in such a way as to deny his deity, but rather affirm both equally, refusing to allow either to contradict the other. In the same way, in our doctrine of Scripture we must neither affirm that it is the Word of God in such a way as to deny that it is the words of human beings (which is fundamentalism), nor affirm that it is the words of human beings in such a way as to deny that it is the Word of God (which is liberalism), but rather affirm both equally, refusing to allow either to contradict the other. Thus, on the one hand, God spoke,[14] determining what he wanted to say, yet without smothering the personality of the human authors. On the other hand, human beings spoke,[15] using their faculties freely, yet without distorting the truth that God was speaking through them.

We have no right to declare that such a combination is impossible. To say so, wrote Dr J. I. Packer, would indicate

> a false doctrine of God, here particularly of his providence . . .
> For it assumes that God and man stand in such a relationship
> to each other that they cannot both be free agents in the same

action. If man acts freely (i.e. voluntarily and spontaneously), God does not, and vice versa. The two freedoms are mutually exclusive. But the affinities of this idea are with Deism, not Christian theism . . . The cure for such fallacious reasoning is to grasp the biblical idea of God's *concursive operation* in, with and through the free working of man's own mind.[16]

The way we understand Scripture will affect the way we read it. In particular, its double authorship demands a double approach. Because Scripture is the Word of God, we should read it as we read no other book – on our knees, humbly, reverently, prayerfully, looking to the Holy Spirit for illumination. But because Scripture is also the words of human beings, we should read it as we read *every* other book, using our minds, thinking, pondering and reflecting, and paying close attention to its literary, historical, cultural and linguistic characteristics. This combination of humble reverence and critical reflection is not only not impossible; it is indispensable.[17]

Third, *Scripture is useful* (verses 16–17). It is able to do more than instruct us for salvation (verse 15); it is also 'useful for teaching, rebuking, correcting and training in righteousness' (verse 16). In other words, it is profitable both for doctrine (teaching truth and correcting error) and for ethics (rebuking sin and training in right living). It leads us on in Christian belief and behaviour until we become men and women of God, 'thoroughly equipped for every good work' (verse 17). In these ways the Bible has an essential part to play in our growth into maturity in Christ, as we will consider more fully in the next chapter. In contrast to the errors of the 'evildoers and impostors', Timothy was to continue in the Word of God, both the Old Testament Scriptures and the apostle's teaching.

Thank God for the Bible! God has not left us to grope our way in the darkness; he has given us a light to show us the path. He has not abandoned us to flounder in heavy seas; Scripture is a rock on which we may stand. Our resolve should be to study it, believe it and obey it.

Preaching the Word

Neither Timothy nor anybody else has the right to monopolize Scripture. For Scripture is nobody's private possession; it is public property. Having been given by God, it belongs to all. His Word has been spoken in order to be passed on. So the apostle, conscious of God's presence and of Christ's future appearing for judgment (4:1), gives Timothy this charge: 'Preach the Word' (verse 2). He must proclaim it like a herald or town crier in the market-place. He must do so boldly, urgently and relevantly, correcting, rebuking and encouraging according to people's state and need, and 'with great patience and careful instruction' (verse 2).

This was all the more necessary, Paul added, because the time was coming when people will 'not put up with sound doctrine'. Instead, suffering from a strange pathological condition called 'itching ears', they will listen to teachers who say what they want to hear, rather than to the truth which God wants to say to them (verses 3–4). Yet the unwillingness of some to listen to the Word of God is no reason why we should give up preaching it! On the contrary, Timothy was to persevere, to keep his head, to endure opposition, and to fulfil his ministry faithfully, both as an evangelist and as a teacher (verse 5).

One of the greatest needs of the contemporary church is conscientious biblical exposition from the pulpit (see chapter 4). Ignorance of even the rudiments of the faith is widespread. Many Christians are immature and unstable. And the major reason for this sorry state of affairs is the scarcity of responsible, thorough, balanced biblical preachers. The pulpit is not the place to air our own opinions, but to unfold God's Word.

The climax of the apostle's exhortation is reached in verses 6–8. In a previous letter, written about two years earlier, he had described himself as 'an old man'.[18] Now he writes that the time of his departure has come. Indeed, the pouring out of his life like a drink offering has already begun (verse 6). Looking back over his apostolic career, he is able to say that he has fought the good fight, finished the race and kept the faith (verse 7). He has no regrets. He is probably incarcerated in the underground Mamertine Prison in Rome, from which he is not expecting to be released. Already with his mind's eye he sees the flash of the executioner's sword, and beyond it 'the crown of righteousness' which on the last day Jesus, the righteous Judge, will give both to him and to 'all who have longed for his appearing' (verse 8). It is this sense that his ministry is nearing its end which prompts him to exhort Timothy to stand firm in the Word, continue in it and pass it on.

I hope it will not be thought too personal if I say that I understand and feel the poignancy of Paul's words, although I do not of course presume to compare myself with him. But as I write these words, I have recently celebrated my seventieth birthday, my statutory 'three score years and ten'.[19] So, naturally, I ask myself, where are the Timothys of the next generation? Where are the young evangelicals, who are determined by God's grace to stand firm in Scripture, refusing to be swept off their feet by the prevailing winds of fashion, who are resolved to continue in it and live by it, relating the Word to the world in order to obey it, and who are committed to passing it on as they give themselves to the ministry of conscientious exposition?

Reflection questions from Tim Chester

1 Do you think of the teaching you have received as 'a sacred deposit to be guarded'? What might this look like in practice?
2 When do you feel pressure from the world around you to compromise on the truth of Scripture?
3 'To read the Bible without meeting Christ is to read it badly.' Do you come to the Bible looking to meet Christ?
4 The Bible's 'double authorship demands a double approach' – a 'combination of humble reverence and critical reflection'. What does it look like for you to read the Bible with humble reverence?

5 What does it look like for you to read the Bible with critical reflection?

6 Both the apostle Paul and John Stott write as men coming to the end of their lives and wanting to see a new generation of Bible people. How would you answer Stott's question, 'Where are the Timothys of the next generation?' Where do you belong in the answer?

2

Responding to the Word

The concept of divine revelation, and of our need to submit to it, is both eminently reasonable and practically wholesome. It is reasonable because it acknowledges that the infinite God is altogether beyond his finite creatures, and that we could never have known him if he had not taken the initiative to make himself known. It is also wholesome because submission to God's self-revelation in Christ and in the full biblical witness to Christ, far from inhibiting the health and growth of the church, is actually indispensable to them.

My claim in this chapter is that God's Word, received and responded to, has a central role in the faith and life of God's people. I will give five examples.

Mature discipleship

First, submission to the authority of Scripture is *the way of mature discipleship*. I am not saying it is impossible to be a disciple of Jesus without a high view of Scripture, for this is manifestly not the case. There are genuine followers of Jesus Christ who are not 'evangelical', whose confidence in Scripture is small, even minimal. Instead, they put more faith in the past traditions and present teaching of the church, or in their own reason or experience. I have no desire to deny the authenticity of their Christian profession. Yet I would add that their discipleship is bound to be impoverished as a result of their attitude to the Bible. A full, balanced and mature Christian discipleship is impossible whenever disciples do not submit to their Lord's teaching authority as it is mediated through Scripture.

For what is discipleship? It is a many-faceted lifestyle, an amalgam of several ingredients. In particular, it includes worship, faith, obedience and hope, as we will see below. Every Christian is called to worship God, to trust and obey him, and to look with confident hope towards the future. Yet each of these is a response to revelation, and is seriously impaired without a reliable, objective revelation of God.

1. *Worship.* Every Christian is a worshipper. In both public and private we recognize our duty to worship Almighty God. But how can we worship God unless we know both who he is and what kind of worship pleases him? Without this knowledge our attempts at worship are almost certain to degenerate into idolatry. At best, we would copy that famous altar which Paul found in Athens and which was inscribed 'TO AN UNKNOWN GOD'.[1] But Christians are not agnostic Athenians; we are to love the Lord our God with all our mind[2] and to worship him 'in the Spirit and in truth'.[3]

What then does it mean to worship God? It is to 'glory in his holy name',[4] that is, to revel adoringly in who he is in his revealed character. But before we can glory in God's name, we must know it. Hence the importance of the reading and preaching of the Word of God in public worship, and of biblical meditation in private devotion. These things are not an intrusion into worship; they form the necessary foundation of it. God must speak to us before we can speak to him. He must disclose to us who he is before we can offer him what we are in acceptable worship. The worship of God is always a response to the Word of God. Scripture wonderfully directs and enriches our worship.

2. *Faith.* If every Christian is a worshipper, every Christian is also a believer. Indeed, the Christian life is a life of faith. 'Where is your faith?' Jesus asked the Twelve when they were afraid, and he exhorted them, 'Have faith in God.'[5]

But what is faith? It too is a response to the revelation of God. We can no more trust a God we do not know than we can worship an unknown God. Consider Psalm 9:10: 'Those who know your name trust in you, for you, LORD, have never forsaken those who seek you.' If worship is to 'glory' in God for who he is (his 'name'), then faith is to 'trust' him because of who he is. So faith is neither naivety nor gullibility. It is neither illogical nor irrational. On the contrary, faith is a reasoning trust. It rests on knowledge, the knowledge of God's name. Its reasonableness arises from the reliability of the God who is being trusted. It is never unreasonable to trust God, since a more trustworthy person does not exist.

Faith will grow therefore as we reflect on the character of God (who never lies) and on the covenant of God (who has pledged himself to his people). But how can we discover his character and covenant? Only from the Bible, in which these twin truths have been revealed. So the more we meditate on God's self-disclosure in Scripture, the more mature our faith will become, whereas without Scripture our faith is bound to be weak and sickly.

3. *Obedience.* Jesus calls his disciples to a life of obedience, as well as one of worship and faith.

But how can we obey him, unless we know his will and commandments? Without a knowledge of these, obedience would be impossible. 'If you love me, keep my commands,' he said.[6] And again, 'Whoever has my commands [that is, knows them, and treasures them up in their mind and memory] and keeps them is the one who loves me.'[7]

Once more, then, the Bible is seen to be indispensable to mature discipleship. For it is there that we learn the commands of Christ, and so take the first necessary step towards understanding and doing his will.

4. *Hope.* The Christian hope is a confident expectation regarding the future. No Christian can be a cynic or a pessimist. It is true that we do not believe human beings will ever succeed in building Utopia on earth. But, although we have little confidence in human achievement, we have great confidence in the purposes and power of God.

We are certain that error and evil are not going to be allowed the last word. On the contrary, truth and righteousness will triumph in the end. For Jesus Christ is going to return in strength and splendour, the dead will be raised, death will be abolished, and the universe will be liberated from decay and saturated with glory.

But how can we be so sure of these things? There are no obvious grounds for such confidence. Evil flourishes. The wicked get away with their wickedness. The problems of the world appear intractable. Global warming overshadows the horizon. Is there not more reason for despair than for hope? Yes, there would be – if it were not for the Bible! It is the Bible which arouses, directs and nurtures hope. For Christian hope is quite different from secular optimism. It is a confidence in God, kindled by the promises of God. 'Let us hold unswervingly to the hope we profess,' the author of Hebrews exhorts his readers. Why? 'For he who promised is faithful.'[8] Jesus himself said that he would come again. 'People will see the Son of Man coming in clouds with great power and glory . . . And you will see the Son of Man . . . coming on the clouds of heaven.'[9] It is promises like these that stimulate our hope. It is 'in keeping with his promise' that we are looking for a new world, in which righteousness will reign.[10]

Here, then, are four basic ingredients of Christian discipleship – worship, faith, obedience and hope. All four would be irrational without an objective basis in God's revelation, to which they are a response:

- worship is a response to the revelation of God's name;
- faith to the revelation of his character and covenant;
- obedience to the revelation of his will and commandments;
- hope to the revelation of his purpose and promises.

And God's name, covenant, commands and promises are all found in Scripture. That is why Scripture is fundamental to Christian growth, and why submission to its authority is the way of mature discipleship.

Intellectual integrity

Second, submission to biblical authority is *the way of intellectual integrity.*

Many people would immediately deny this statement and even affirm the contrary. They cannot understand how apparently intelligent Christians in the modern era can possibly be so perverse as to believe in biblical inspiration and authority. They regard a commitment to the truth and trustworthiness of Scripture as untenable. They therefore charge those of us who hold to this with a lack of intellectual integrity. They accuse us of deliberate vagueness, mental schizophrenia, intellectual suicide and other equally horrid conditions. To these charges, however, we plead 'not guilty'. We insist that our conviction about Scripture arises from the very integrity which our critics say we lack.

'Integrity' is the quality of an integrated person. In particular, integrated Christians are at peace, not at war, with themselves. Instead of being conscious of a dichotomy between our various beliefs, or between our beliefs and our behaviour, so that we are 'torn apart' inside, there is an inner harmony. We are 'all of a piece', or whole. What is the secret of this integration?

There is no more integrating Christian principle than the affirmation that 'Jesus Christ is Lord'. The essence of integrated discipleship is that we both confess his lordship with our lips and enthrone him as Lord in our hearts. We assume the easy yoke of his teaching authority.[11] We seek to 'take captive every thought to make it obedient to Christ'.[12] And when Jesus is Lord of our beliefs, opinions, ambitions, standards, values and lifestyle, then we are integrated Christians, and 'integrity' marks our life. Only when *he* is Lord do *we* become whole.

But Jesus our Lord himself submitted to the Old Testament Scriptures. In his ethical conduct, in his understanding of his mission and in his public debates with contemporary religious leaders, his primary concern was to be true to Scripture. 'What does the Scripture say?' he would ask. It was always his final court of appeal. And he expected his disciples to follow his example in this. He also made provision for the Scriptures of the New Testament to be written, by choosing, calling, equipping and commissioning his apostles to be the teachers of the church, and he expected the church to submit to them. 'Whoever listens to you listens to me,' he said.[13] As a result of this, submission to Scripture by Christian disciples is part and parcel of our submission to Jesus as Lord. For the disciple is not above his teacher. So we cannot let ourselves be comfortable with selective submission. It would be inherently illogical, for example, to agree with Jesus' doctrine of God, but disagree with his view of the Word of God. No, selective submission is not authentic submission.

This gives us the clue we need regarding how to deal with the problems in the Bible. For in affirming the inspiration and authority of Scripture, I am not denying that there are problems. There are textual, literary, historical, scientific, philosophical, cultural, theo-logical and moral problems. The observable phenomena of Scripture (which we see inductively in the pages of the Bible) sometimes seem to conflict with our doctrine of Scripture (which we hold deductively, inferring it from the attitude and teaching of Jesus). So what should we do with problems? How can we handle them with integrity?

We need to remember that every Christian doctrine raises problems. This includes the central doctrines of God (his being, creation, sovereignty, providence and justice), of Jesus Christ (his one person in two natures, his work of atonement, his bodily resur-rection, present reign and future return) and of the Holy Spirit (his activity in the church and the world). Or take the love of God. It is a fundamental Christian doctrine. Every Christian without exception believes that God is love (Roman Catholic, Orthodox, Reformed, Lutheran, Episcopal, Independent, Pentecostal). If they denied it, they would not be Christians. Yet the problems surrounding this belief are enormous: for example, the origin and spread of evil, the suffering of the innocent, the 'silences' of God and the 'acts' of God, the vastness of the universe, and the apparent insignificance of individual human beings.

Supposing somebody comes to us with a personal problem or dilemma (perhaps the birth of a disabled child, a natural disaster or a tragic bereavement) and challenges us: 'Why should this happen to me? How can God be love if he allows this?' How do we react? Do we say that, in order to preserve our intellectual integrity, we must suspend our belief in the love of God until we have solved the problem? I hope not. Nor do we sweep the problem under the carpet and try to forget it. No, instead, in addition to the question of how we should respond pastorally to our questioner, we wrestle with the problem in our own mind and heart. We think about it conscientiously, read about it, talk about it and pray about it. And during this process some light is thrown upon the problem. Yet some of the perplexity remains. So what next? The way of intellectual integrity, I suggest, is to retain our conviction about God's love, in spite of the remaining difficulties, ultimately for one reason only, namely that Jesus our Lord himself taught it and exhibited it. It was because of Jesus that we came to believe in God's love in the first place; it is for the same reason that we should continue to do so.

It is the same with problems relating to the Bible. We need to learn to face them as we face problems surrounding other Christian doctrines. If somebody comes to us with a biblical problem (a discrepancy, for example, between theology and science, or between two Gospel accounts, or a moral dilemma), what should we do? We should not (from a mistaken form of integrity) suspend our belief in the truth of Scripture until we have solved the problem. Nor should we place the problem on a shelf (indefinitely postponing its challenge) or under a carpet (permanently concealing it, even from ourselves). Instead, we should struggle conscientiously with the problem in thought, discussion and prayer. As we do so, some difficulties may be wholly or partly cleared up. But then, in spite of those which remain, we should retain our belief about Scripture on the ground that Jesus himself taught and exhibited it.

If a critic says to me, 'You are an anti-intellectual to believe the Bible to be the Word of God in defiance of the problems', I now return the compliment and say, 'OK, if you like, I am. But then you are an anti-intellectual to believe in the love of God in defiance of the problems.' Actually, however, to believe a Christian doctrine in spite of its problems, because of the acknowledged lordship of Jesus Christ, is not obscurantism (preferring darkness to light), but faith (trusting him who said he was the light of the world). It is more than faith; it is the sober, intellectual integrity of confessing Jesus as Lord.

Ecumenical progress

Third, submission to the authority of Scripture is *the way of ecumenical progress*, that is to say, the means by which to secure an acceptable coming together of churches.

Now I realize that some of my readers may have no desire to make any such progress. You may be (I am guessing) suspicious of the whole ecumenical movement. You can see (although it is always misleading to generalize) its tendency to doctrinal indifference, its attempt to reinterpret Christian mission in terms of socio-political action, and its leaning towards syncretism and universalism in the face of other faiths. Indeed, I understand your concerns, for I share them. There is much in contemporary ecumenism to perplex and even distress us.

Nevertheless, I am also disturbed by the blanket condemnation of ecumenical activity expressed by a large section of the evangelical constituency. It is clear to me that we cannot simply dismiss the whole non-evangelical section of Christianity as if it did not exist, or, since it does exist, regard it as non-Christian and resolve to have nothing to do with it. Jesus our Lord prayed that his people might be one, in order that the world might believe,[14] and his apostle Paul urges us to 'make every effort to keep the unity of the Spirit through the bond of peace'.[15]

There is, of course, room for disagreement among us regarding what shape Christian unity should take. But it should be possible to agree that competition between different churches is inappropriate, and that the visible unity of the church in some form is a desirable goal. In his reply to a letter from Thomas Cranmer, Archbishop of Canterbury, in 1552, John Calvin wrote as follows:

> Doubtless it must be counted among the greatest misfortunes of our century that churches are thus separated from each other ... and that the holy communion of the members of Christ, which many confess with their mouth, is only sincerely sought after by few ... From this it follows that the members being so scattered, the body of the church lies bleeding. This affects me so deeply, that, if anybody could see that I might be of any use, I should not hesitate to cross ten seas for this business, if that were needful ... Indeed, if learned men were to seek a solid and carefully devised agreement according to the rule of Scripture, an agreement by which the separated churches should unite with each other, I think that for my part I ought not to spare any trouble or dangers.[16]

Calvin's letter to Cranmer is significant, not only because of the goal he had in view (the uniting of separated churches), but also because of the means he proposed (agreement according to the rule of Scripture). For the unity Christ himself desires for his church is certainly a unity in truth. His prayer recorded in John 17 clearly links the two. The church is built on the foundation of the apostles and prophets, with Christ himself as the chief cornerstone,[17] and it will certainly not grow in size or stability by neglecting, let alone undermining, its foundation.

The one apostolic faith that unites us has, of course, come down to us in the New Testament, and no union of churches could or should be contemplated which deviates from this rule. In particular, one of the greatest obstacles to unity has been the failure to distinguish between Scripture and tradition. Jesus himself drew a clear distinction between written Scripture and the oral tradition of the elders, making the latter subordinate to the former, and even went so far as to reject tradition as 'human rules' so that Scripture as the Word of God might have the supremacy.[18] The very same distinction needs to be made today. Yet an example of why some church unity schemes have failed is the tendency of Anglican or Episcopal churches to insist on a particular view of the 'historic episcopate' (church government through bishops) as non-negotiable. One can understand the historical reasons for this, and I myself would want to defend an episcopal form of government as a pastoral ideal that is consistent with Scripture and conducive to the health of the church. But one cannot insist on it as indispensable, since it belongs to the tradition of the church, and is not required by Scripture.

If only we could agree that Scripture is 'God's Word written' (Anglican Article XX), that it is supreme in its authority over all human traditions, however venerable, and that it must be allowed to reform and renew the church, we would take an immediate leap forward in ecumenical relationships. Reformation according to the Word of God is indispensable to reunion.

Effective evangelism

Fourth, submission to the authority of Scripture is *the way of faithful and effective evangelism*. My argument so far has been domestic and ecclesiastical, as we have thought about personal discipleship and church relations. All the time the world outside is in great confusion and darkness. Has the church any light for this darkness, any word of hope for the bewildered modern world?

One of the tragedies of the contemporary church is that just when the world seems to be ready to listen, the church often seems to have little to say. For the church itself is confused. It shares the current bewilderment, instead of addressing it. The church is insecure, uncertain of its identity, mission and message. It stammers and stutters when it should be proclaiming the gospel with boldness. Indeed, the major reason for its diminishing influence in the West is its diminishing faith.

A recovery of evangelism is impossible without a recovery of the *evangel*, 'the good news'. For evangelism, according to its simplest definition, is 'sharing the evangel'. So biblical evangelism is impossible without the biblical evangel. Evangelism has to be defined in terms of the evangel itself.

We should be able to agree that Christian witness is essentially witness to Christ, and that the only authentic Christ is the Christ of the apostolic witness. For the apostles were the original witnesses, the eyewitnesses, so our witness, vital though it is, always remains secondary to theirs. We have no authority to edit their gospel. Our calling is rather to preserve it like stewards, proclaim it like heralds and argue it like advocates.

In his book *Go and Make Disciples*, David Read, the former minister of Madison Avenue Presbyterian Church in New York, wrote, 'Those of us who enjoy visiting other countries are familiar with that solemn moment when at the frontier we encounter a customs official who . . . fixes us with steely eyes and asks "Have you anything to declare?" I have not yet had the nerve to answer "Yes, as a minister of the gospel, it is my duty to declare that Jesus Christ is your Lord and Saviour".' So David Read calls his final chapter 'The Crux: Have You Anything to Declare?' It is lack of conviction about the gospel, he writes, which makes 'most of us . . . reluctant evangelists'.[19]

I agree. I think there is no chance of the church taking its evangelistic task seriously unless it first recovers its confidence in the truth, relevance and power of the gospel, and begins to get excited about it again. For this, however, it will have to return to the Bible in which the gospel has been revealed.

Personal humility

Fifth, submission to the authority of Scripture is *the way of personal Christian humility.* Nothing is more obnoxious in those of us who claim to follow Jesus Christ than arrogance, and nothing is more appropriate or attractive than humility. And an essential element in Christian humility is the willingness to hear and receive God's Word. Perhaps the greatest of all our needs is to take our place again humbly, quietly and expectantly at the feet of Jesus Christ, in order to listen attentively to his Word, and to believe and obey it. For we have no freedom to disbelieve or disobey him.

The ultimate issue before us and the whole church is whether Jesus Christ is Lord (as we say he is) or not. The question is whether Christ is Lord of the church (to teach and command it), or the church is lord of Christ (to edit and manipulate his teaching). In the contemporary crisis of authority in the world, and loss of authority in the church, my plea is that we return to a humble submission to Scripture as God's Word. We must submit to Scripture out of a humble submission to Jesus Christ as Lord, who himself humbly submitted to Scripture in his own faith, life, mission and teaching.

In so doing, we will find the way of mature discipleship and intellectual integrity, the way to unite churches and evangelize the world, and the way to express a proper humility before our Lord Jesus Christ. That is what I mean by the 'wholesomeness' of submitting to the authority of Scripture.

Reflections questions from Tim Chester

1 Can you think of specific ways in which your worship, faith, obedience or hope have recently been shaped by God's Word?

2 What 'problems' do you face as you read the Bible or share its message? How can you respond to these in an integrated way?

3 Can you think of beliefs and practices in your church which are not required by Scripture (though they may be consistent with Scripture)? Have these ever become a barrier to working with other Christians?

4 What is the link between confidence in the gospel and commitment to evangelism? What could you do to become or remain excited about the gospel?

5 Claiming that Christianity is *the* truth is often seen as arrogant. Why can it actually be a sign of humility?

6 How would you explain why it is 'wholesome' to submit to Scripture?

3
Transposing the Word

Whenever we pick up the Bible and read it, even in a contemporary version, we are conscious of stepping back two millennia or more. We travel backwards in time, behind the information revolution and the Industrial Revolution, until we find ourselves in an alien world that long ago ceased to exist. As a result, the Bible feels odd, sounds archaic, looks obsolete and smells musty. We are tempted to ask impatiently, 'What on earth has that old book got to say to me?'

Our sense of disorientation when we read the Bible, and the resulting difficulty we experience understanding it, are due primarily neither to the passage of time in itself (from the first century to the twenty-first) nor to the mere distance (from the Middle East to the West), but to the cultural differences which remoteness of time and place have caused.

In fact, two distinct but complementary problems confront us. The first is the problem of our own cultural imprisonment, and the second is the problem of the cultural conditioning of the biblical authors. That is, both the writers and the readers of Scripture are culture-creatures, the products (and therefore to some degree the prisoners) of the particular cultures in which they were brought up. As a result, in all our Bible reading there is a collision of cultures between the biblical world and the modern world. Both God's speaking and our listening are culturally conditioned. This fact clearly affects our *interpretation* of Scripture. But we will have to ask whether it also affects the *authority* of Scripture.

The hermeneutical problem

Biblical hermeneutics, the art or science of interpreting Scripture, has become a major preoccupation of scholars in recent decades. Indeed, all Christians who read the Bible come up against the question of how to understand it rightly.

The problem arises from the extreme cultural particularities of the ancient text and the modern interpreter. Each has a different 'horizon', a limited viewpoint or perspective, and what is needed is what Hans-Georg Gadamer called a 'fusion' of horizons. 'Understanding takes place,' writes Dr Tony Thiselton in his classic and comprehensive study *The Two Horizons*,[1] 'when two sets of horizons are brought into relation to each other, namely those of the text and those of the interpreter.'[2]

In this process the interpreter's first task was called by Gadamer 'distancing'. This means we have to acknowledge 'the pastness of the past', disengage ourselves from the text, and allow it its own historical integrity. We must avoid letting ourselves intrude into it or deciding prematurely how it applies to us. Careful exegesis of the text necessitates studying it on its own cultural and linguistic terms.

But this is only the beginning. If first we stand back from the text, next we seek to enter it. 'There must be present engagement with the text,' writes Tony Thiselton, 'as well as critical distancing from it.'[3] This is not easy, because the interpreter also belongs to a particular context, one that is different from that of the text. It requires a high degree of imagination, of empathy, if we are to enter that alien world. 'Historical exegesis is essential, but it is not enough. We need *both* distancing *and* an openness to the text which will yield progress towards the fusion of horizons.'[4]

This leads to an active interaction between text and interpreter. However hard we may work at distancing ourselves from the text, we can hardly help bringing to it our presuppositions and our own agenda of problems and questions. The Scripture may respond to these. But, because it has its own agenda, it may not. Instead, it may challenge us to go away and reshape our questions, even replace them with better ones. We then return with our new agenda, and so the dialogue between us goes on. It is part of what is called 'the hermeneutical circle', although some European and Latin American scholars have preferred the expression 'hermeneutical spiral' because the movement is progressive and upward.[5]

During the 1960s, some German scholars, especially Ernst Fuchs and Gerhard Ebeling, former students of Rudolf Bultmann, went further in developing a 'new hermeneutic'. They claimed that objectivity is impossible on the grounds that we cannot jump out of our own particular situation into that of a biblical author. Instead, they stressed the need to let the text speak. According to their theory of language, its purpose is not so much to convey 'concepts' as to cause an 'event' (a 'language-event'). The roles of text and interpreter are reversed, with the interpreter listening instead of talking. It seems clear that these post-Bultmannians went too far. Denying that the biblical text has an accessible, objective meaning, they lapsed into an uncontrolled subjectivity. What the text said to them might bear no relation to what it actually meant.

Nevertheless, there is abiding value in what these scholars are feeling for. They take seriously the cultural gulf between the past and the present. They recognize the independent historical particularity of both text and interpreter, and they seek to develop a dialectic between them. The old hermeneutic put into our hands a set of universal rules of interpretation, which we applied to the text; the new hermeneutic is concerned to allow the text to apply its message to us. The old hermeneutic concentrated on the text as *object* – an object that we stood over, studied, scrutinized, applied our rules to, and almost took control of. The new hermeneutic, however, concentrates on the text as *subject*. The text stands over us, and we sit meekly 'under it', as the Reformers used to put it. It addresses, confronts, challenges and changes us.

Here, then, is the danger of a new polarization between the 'old' and the 'new'. Each is perilously lopsided without the other. For the text is both object and subject. We address it, and it addresses us. But as these two processes develop, we must insist that the object and the subject are the same text and have the same meaning.

We now return to the two cultural problems, and consider each separately.

Our own cultural imprisonment

Every human being who has ever lived has been a creature of culture. Culture is a convenient term with which to describe the complexity of beliefs, values, customs and traditions which each generation receives from its predecessor and transmits to its successor, and which binds a society together. We have all drunk in our cultural inheritance with our mother's milk. The way we think, judge, act, talk, dress, eat, work and play are all to a large extent determined by our culture, and we usually do not realize how much our cultural upbringing has enslaved us.

Hence the great value of travel, for then we learn to listen to ourselves through the ears of another culture, and look at ourselves through another culture's eyes. I well remember my first visit to the United States. After the first address I had given on American soil, a woman said to me, 'I do like your English accent.' Accent? Me? She of course had an American accent, but surely I spoke the Queen's English? My speech was the norm; hers was the deviation from the norm. Then, not so long afterwards, I was in Manila, and a little Filipino boy of only about eight years old came up to me, cocked his head, looked into my face and commented cheekily, 'You *do* talk funny!' He was right. I do. But then so do you, and so does everybody.

Our culture includes not only the general views and values, standards and customs, of our society, but also those which apply to our particular sex, age and class. They all affect the way we read the Bible. For example, how can I, as a man, read Scripture in the same way as a woman who has been hurt by male chauvinism? Or how can I, as an old man, hear from Scripture what young people hear when they read it? Or again, how can I, as a member of an affluent society, really listen to what Scripture says about the poor?

Men and women, old and young, black and white, African and Asian, capitalist and socialist, waged and unwaged, middle-class and working-class, all read Scripture differently. Our spectacles have cultural lenses. It is so difficult, as to be almost impossible, for us to read the Bible with genuine objectivity and openness, and for God to break through our cultural defences and to say to us what he wants to say. Instead, we come to our reading of the Bible with our own agenda, bias, questions, preoccupations, concerns and convictions, and, unless we are extremely careful, we impose these on the biblical text. We may sincerely pray before we read, 'Open my eyes that I may see wonderful things in your law,'[6] but still the same failure of communication may continue. For even that introductory prayer, even though it is taken from the Psalter, is suspect because it lays down the kind of message we want to hear.

'Please, Lord, I want to see some "wonderful thing" in your Word.'

But he may reply, 'What makes you think I have only "wonderful things" to show you? As a matter of fact, I have some rather "disturbing things" to show you today. Are you prepared to receive them?'

'Oh no, Lord, please not,' we stammer in reply. 'I come to Scripture only to be comforted. I really do not want to be challenged or disturbed.'

In other words, we come to the Bible with our agenda formulated by us alone, our expectations pre-set, our minds made up, laying down in advance what we want God to say to us. Then, instead of hearing the thunderclap of his voice, all we receive are the soothing echoes of our own cultural prejudice. And God says to us, as he did to his servant through Isaiah, 'Hear, you deaf; look, you blind, and see! Who is blind but my servant, and deaf like the messenger I send?'[7]

This explains the dismal record of the church's unfaithfulness. Seldom in its long history has it been sensitively in tune with God's Word. More often it has been exactly what it has been forbidden to be, namely conformist.[8] It has been influenced more by the world than by the Word. Instead of challenging the status quo with the values of the kingdom of God, it has acquiesced in it. Instead of resisting the encroachments of secularism, it has surrendered to them. Instead of rejecting the value system and lifestyle of the world, it has assimilated them. The church has accommodated itself to the prevailing culture, leaped on all the trendiest bandwagons, and hummed all the popular tunes of the day. Whenever the church does this, it reads Scripture through the world's eyes, and rationalizes its own unfaithfulness.

Is this unfair? I do not think so. Consider some examples from the past. For church history is full of the church's cultural blind spots.

How is it, I ask myself, that the Christian conscience not only approved, but actually glamorized, those terrible medieval Crusades as a Christ-glorifying form of mission, so that European Christian knights in shining armour rode forth to recover the holy places from Islam by force? It was an unholy blunder, which Muslims have never forgotten, let alone forgiven, and which continues to obstruct the evangelization of the Muslim world, especially in the Middle East. Or how is it that torture could ever have been employed in the name of Jesus Christ to combat heresy and enforce orthodoxy, so that the thumbscrews were turned on some miserable dissident until he capitulated? One might almost characterize it 'evangelization by torture', and all in the name of the Prince of Peace! Or how is that, although the Franciscans organized missions in the thirteenth century, and the Jesuits in the sixteenth, Protestant churches were so inward looking that they had virtually no missions until the time of the Pietists two centuries after the Reformation? Even then, towards the end of the eighteenth century, when William Carey proposed a mission to India, he was greeted with the patronizing retort, 'Sit down, young man; when God wants to convert the heathen, he will do it without your help or mine.' Had his critic never read the Great Commission? Again, how is it that the cruel degradations of slavery and of the slave trade were not abolished in the so-called Christian West until 1,800 years after Christ? Or how is it that racial prejudice and environmental pollution have become widely recognized as the evils they are only since the Second World War?

This is a catalogue of some of the worst blind spots that have marred the church's testimony down the ages. None of them can be defended from Scripture, although tortuous attempts have been made to do so. All are due to a misreading of Scripture or to an unwillingness to sit under its authority. God's people were blinded by tradition. They had other agendas. They were not in a mind or mood to listen to God.

What then about our own contemporary blindness? It is comparatively easy to criticize our forebears for their blindness; it is much harder to be aware of ours. What will posterity see as the chief Christian blind spot in our day? I cannot say with any degree of certainty, because of course I share in the same myopia myself. But I suspect that it will relate to two main areas.

First, we Christians who live in the affluence of the West still do not seem to have felt sufficiently the injustice of continuing North-South economic inequality. Quite apart from macro-economic questions of trade and development, we do not even seem to have allowed the situation to affect our lifestyle. While about 20,000 people die of poverty each day,[9] should not the Christian voice of protest be louder and more strident? And should we not continue to simplify our own economic lifestyle, not because we imagine that this will solve the problem, but because it will enable us personally to share more, and to express appropriately our sense of compassionate solidarity with the poor?

A second blind spot of evangelical Christians seems to me to be our comparative failure to condemn as immoral and indefensible all indiscriminate weaponry – both those that are indiscriminate by nature like nuclear, biological and chemical weapons, as well as the indiscriminate use of conventional weapons. We should surely be denouncing this as incompatible with the 'just war' theory, let alone with Christian pacifism. It was back in 1965 that the Roman Catholic Church condemned such weapons as 'a crime against God and man himself'. Ecumenical pronouncements followed, declaring indiscriminate warfare 'increasingly offensive to the Christian conscience'. But the evangelical voice, with notable exceptions, has been irresponsibly muted.

The first step towards the recovery of our Christian integrity will be the humble recognition that our culture blinds, deafens and dopes us. We neither see what we ought to see in Scripture, nor hear God's Word as we should, nor feel the anger of God against evil. We need to allow God's Word to confront us, disturbing our security, undermining our complacency, penetrating our protective patterns of thought and behaviour, and overthrowing our resistance.

It is not impossible for God to do this. Once we realize how strong a barrier to his communication our culture can be, we will be alert to the problem. Then we will begin to cry to him to open our eyes, unstop our ears and stab our dull consciences awake, until we see, hear and feel what (through his Word) God has been saying to us all the time.

The Bible's cultural conditioning

It is not only Bible readers who are the products of a particular culture; so too were the biblical authors. And God took this into account when he communicated with his people. That is, when he spoke, he neither used his own language (if he has one), nor expressed himself in terms of his own heavenly culture. Such communication would have been unintelligible to human beings on earth. Nor did God shout culture-free maxims out of a clear, blue sky. On the contrary, he humbled himself to speak in the languages of his people (classical Hebrew, Aramaic and common Greek), and within the cultures of the Ancient Near East (the Old Testament), Palestinian Judaism (the Gospels) and the Hellenized Roman Empire (the rest of the New Testament). No word of God was spoken in a cultural vacuum; every word of God was spoken in a cultural context.

True, the cultural contexts in which the Bible was written are often alien to us. But we must not resent this on the grounds that it causes us problems. We should rather rejoice in the divine condescension. God has stooped to our level in order to reveal himself in linguistically and culturally appropriate terms. This truth applies both to the incarnation of his Son, who took human flesh, and to the inspiration of his Word, which was spoken in human language.

Nevertheless, we are also faced with this question: how can a divine revelation given in transient cultural terms have permanent validity? How can a revelation addressed to a particular cultural situation have a universal application? Does not the cultural conditioning of Scripture limit its relevance to us, and even its authority over us? Must we not say with David Edwards, 'I admit that a lot in the Bible . . . is culturally conditioned, and therefore out of date'?[10] Is his deduction logical?

My response to David Edwards is to agree that the Bible is a culturally conditioned book (as indeed are all books which have ever been written, including his and mine!), but to disagree that it is therefore necessarily out of date. How then shall we handle the cultural element in Scripture?

The principle, as I see it, can be set out through an everyday illustration. We have little difficulty in distinguishing between a person and the particular clothing that he or she happens to be wearing. Most of us have several sets of clothes at home. Sometimes we dress up in maximum finery, for a wedding or party perhaps, or in our national costume. At other times we put on more sombre clothing, as when we attend a funeral. Occasionally we dress up in archaic garments, perhaps when going to a fancy-dress party. We also have our work clothes, our sports clothes and our night clothes. In other words, there is variety in our wardrobe. But the person underneath the clothing remains the same. The clothing changes; the person does not.

Now, just as we distinguish between individuals and their clothing, so we need to distinguish between the essence of God's revelation (what he is teaching, promising or commanding) and the cultural clothing in which it was originally given. However dated the cultural setting may be, the essential message has permanent and universal validity. The cultural application may change; the revelation does not.

When we are faced with a biblical passage, therefore, whose teaching is obviously clothed in ancient cultural dress (because it relates to social customs that are either obsolete or at least alien to our own culture), how shall we react? We have three options.

The first possibility is *total rejection*. 'Because the culture is out of date,' we could say to ourselves, 'the teaching here is irrelevant. It has nothing to say to me. I may as well take a pair of scissors, cut this passage out of my Bible, and throw it away.' I am not recommending this response!

The second and opposite possibility is *wooden, unimaginative literalism*. The literalist says, 'Because this text is part of God's Word, it must be preserved and followed just as it stands, without modification. Both the substance and its cultural expression have equal authority. To discard either would be to tamper with the Word of God and be guilty of an incipient liberalism.' I do not recommend this response either.

There is a third and more judicious way, which is called *cultural transposition*. The procedure now is to identify the essential revelation in the text (what God is saying here), to separate this from the cultural form in which he chose to give it, and then to re-clothe it in appropriate modern cultural terms. 'Transposition' is a good word for this practice, since we are already familiar with it in musical contexts. To transpose a piece of music is to put it into a different key from that in which it was originally written. To transpose a biblical text is to put it into a different culture from that in which it was originally given. In musical transposition the tune and harmonization remain the same; only the key is different. In biblical transposition the truth of the revelation remains the same; only the cultural expression is different.

Cross-cultural missionaries illustrate the need for cultural transposition, although they have to wrestle with three cultures. Their task is to take the essence of the gospel, which was first revealed in the cultural settings of the Bible, which they have received in their own cultures, and transpose it into the culture of the people to whom they go. And they need to do so without thereby either falsifying the message or rendering it unintelligible.[11] That, at least, is the theory. In practice, missionaries have often taken with them what Dr René Padilla at the Lausanne Congress in 1974 called a 'culture-Christianity'. In other words, they exported with the gospel their own cultural inheritance.

I remember the shock I felt on my first visit to West Africa and its churches. I saw Gothic spires rising incongruously above the coconut palms, and African bishops sweating profusely in the tropical heat because they were wearing medieval European ecclesiastical robes. I heard Western hymn tunes being sung to the accompaniment of Western instruments, and African tongues attempting to get around Jacobean and even Elizabethan English! It is, of course, easy to criticize, and, if we had been in the position of the early missionaries, we would probably have made the same mistake. Nevertheless, this imposition of Western cultural forms was a serious blunder. What is needed instead is what Stanley Jones in India called the 'naturalization' of the gospel,[12] which means its transposition into indigenous cultural forms.

Looking again at the three options before us, we might perhaps say that

- 'total rejection' is to throw out the baby with the bathwater;
- 'wooden literalism' is to keep both the baby and the bathwater;
- 'cultural transposition' is to keep the baby and change the bathwater.

Examples of cultural transposition

The Bible is concerned about both doctrine and ethics, belief and behaviour, and in both areas cultural transposition is necessary.

Take first the doctrinal or theological teaching of the Bible. It seems obvious that we must learn to distinguish between the truth being affirmed, and the cultural terms in which it is presented; between meaning (the revelation) and medium (its communication). It is in this connection that we have to face the challenge posed by the German scholar Rudolf Bultmann and his 'demythologization' programme, which continues to shape the way many liberal churches read the Bible. Bultmann's argument may be reduced to three points without too much distortion, relating respectively to the biblical authors, their modern readers and theological communicators. First, he argued that the intellectual framework of the biblical writers was pre-scientific and therefore 'mythical'. For example, they envisaged heaven above and hell below in a three-decker universe, so that they imagined Jesus literally 'descending to hell' and 'ascending to heaven'. Second, if modern scientific men and women are presented today with the gospel (*kerygma*) couched in terms of such an obsolete cosmology, they will reject it as, frankly, incredible. Third, the task of theologians is therefore to strip away the mythical elements in the Bible, or 'demythologize the *kerygma*', because the purpose of myth is to speak not of historical events but of transcendent reality.

Let us agree at once with the spirit of the second point above. Our priority concern is how to communicate the *kerygma* to people today in a way that is credible. In order to do so, we have to proclaim biblical *truth*, but not necessarily use biblical *terms*. We may (and must) transpose revealed truth into modern idiom.

With regard to Bultmann's first point, however, I am not myself at all convinced that the biblical authors were the literalists he imagines. It is true that they used the imagery of the three-decker universe, for it was part of their intellectual framework. But were they actually affirming it? I think not. Take Psalm 75. God is said, when the earth quakes, to 'hold its pillars firm'.[13] So here is the earth (the middle deck) resting on pillars. But in the same psalm God commands the wicked not to lift up their 'horns' or these will be cut off,[14] and warns that in his hand there is 'a cup full of foaming wine mixed with spices', which he will shortly pour out for the wicked to drink.[15] Now nobody (least of all the psalmist) believed literally that the wicked sprout horns or that God holds a cup of wine in his hand. If, therefore, these are examples of dramatic, poetic imagery, is it not gratuitous to insist that the earth's pillars are meant to be understood literally?

The Old Testament writers affirmed God's sovereign control of the world by saying that he held earth's pillars firm, without committing themselves to a three-decker cosmology. They affirmed God's power over evil by referring to his destruction of the primeval monster Leviathan,[16] without committing themselves to the Babylonian creation myth. They also affirmed his general revelation through nature by saying that the sun runs across the sky,[17] without committing themselves to a pre-Copernican universe. These forms of thought and speech, whether we call them 'imagery', 'poetry' or 'myth', were common currency in the Ancient Near East. Old

Testament writers used them to convey truths about God as Creator and Lord, without affirming the literal truth of the imagery or mythology they were using.

This brings us to Bultmann's third point. We should be able to agree with the need, in some degree, to 'demythologize', if what is meant is the need to transpose truth from one set of images to another, as we have just seen. But Bultmann goes much further than this, especially in relation to the New Testament. He attempts to reconstruct the *kerygma* (especially the death, resurrection and return of Jesus) by dissolving these historical events into a 'meaning' that is not historical. Thus, according to Bultmann, when the apostles said that 'Christ died for our sins', they were not referring to any literal sin-bearing sacrifice, but affirming God's love and our own existential experience of being crucified with Christ. When they said that 'he rose', they were referring not to an event, but to an experience, namely that he rose in their own revived faith. And when they said that he is coming again to judge, they were referring not to a future event, but to a present challenge to make a responsible decision for Christ today.

The key question, however, is whether the affirmations that Christ died, rose and will return were deliberately mythical ways of referring to something other than historical events, or whether they were real happenings which were themselves part of the *kerygma* being proclaimed. The natural interpretation of the apostolic *kerygma* is that the apostles intended to proclaim events in the career of Jesus which were both historically true and theologically significant.

It is, then, legitimate to distinguish between the meaning and the medium, between what is being affirmed and how the affirmation is made, between the revelation of truth and its communication. But it is also essential to ask whether the words and images used are literal or mythical. The defeat of Leviathan is a myth; the death, resurrection and coming of Jesus belong to history. The intention of the author will usually help us to know which is which.

We turn now to three examples of cultural transposition in the ethical field.

I will begin with a fairly easy example of foot-washing, so that we may firmly grasp the principle and its application. After Jesus had washed the feet of the Twelve in the upper room and resumed his place, he said, 'Now that I, your Lord and Teacher, have washed your feet, you also should wash one another's feet.'[18] In Jesus' day, foot-washing was a common cultural practice. If we had been invited to a meal in a friend's house, we would have walked there barefoot or in sandals through dusty streets, and when we arrived a slave would have washed our feet. Today, however, at least in the West, the whole culture has changed. We visit a friend by car or public transport. On arrival, there is certainly no slave to meet us and wash our feet. How then shall we handle a text in which reciprocal foot-washing is commanded?

Think of the three options. Shall we go the way of total rejection, on the ground that foot-washing has no place in our culture? No. Shall we obey Jesus' command literally, and go round asking people to take their shoes and socks off so that we may wash their feet? No. Although the Mennonites, and some African and Asian churches, have a ritual foot-washing as part of their communion service, it seems clear that Jesus' reference was to a social custom, not to a religious ceremony. We are left then with the third option of cultural transposition. We ask what Jesus was getting at, what was the essence of his instruction. The answer is not hard to find. He was teaching that if we love one another, we must serve one another, and no service will be too dirty, menial or demeaning for us to perform. If, then, we cannot wash people's feet, we will gladly shine their shoes, or wash the dishes for them, or even clean the toilets. Nothing will be beneath our dignity. Whatever in our culture is regarded as unpleasant work of low status, *that* will be our privilege, out of love, to undertake.

A second example of the need for cultural transposition relates to the eating of meat offered to idols.[19] The question was whether it was permissible for the followers of Jesus to eat the meat of animals, which, before being put on sale in a butcher's shop, had been offered in an idolatrous sacrifice. New converts, freshly rescued from heathen idolatry, had conscientious qualms about doing so. Would not the eating of idol meats contaminate and compromise them? Paul was clear that it would not. Idols were nothing, he said. There was only one God, the Father, and only one Lord, Jesus Christ.[20] So he saw no reason why he should not eat idol meats. His conscience was 'strong', that is, well educated. But then there were the 'weak' believers to consider. Their 'weakness' was not in their will but in their conscience, which was under-educated and therefore over-scrupulous. If Paul were to eat meat previously offered to idols in their presence, they might be encouraged to follow his example against their better judgment, in which case their conscience would be defiled. As a result, out of deference to the weak Christians, Paul refrained.

This heated controversy in the New Testament sounds very alien to our context, at least in the West. There are no pagan temples in our culture where animals are sacrificed to idols, nor are there any meat markets in which we could buy food which had been used in idolatrous worship. Yet at least two principles remain, which were laid down by Paul, and which are relevant to Christians in every culture today. The first is that conscience is sacred. To be sure, it needs to be educated. But, even when it is weak, it must not be violated. 'Conscientious objection' not only to military service, but in other situations as well, is allowed in those countries which have had a Christian influence. Second, love limits liberty. Paul had liberty of conscience to eat, but he denied himself this freedom out of loving concern for those who would be offended if he did. These two principles can be applied in many different cultural contexts today.

My third example is the most controversial. It concerns the position and roles of women. Whole books have been written on this topic. I can hope here only to consider how far cultural transposition may be appropriate and helpful in this area. We are familiar both with Paul's prohibitions, that a woman may not 'teach or . . . assume authority over a man',[21] and with his commands, that women are to wear veils and remain silent in public worship.[22] The question that these texts raise is this: are all these instructions of permanent and universal validity? Or do they contain some cultural elements which could allow us a little flexibility in interpretation, and which may need transposition into our own culture? My response necessitates first making two affirmations and then asking two more questions.

The first affirmation is that the sexes are equal. This is taught in Genesis 1:26–28. Men and women are equal bearers of the divine image, and equal sharers in the earthly dominion. Moreover, if they are equal by creation, they are even more equal (if that is possible) by redemption. For in Jesus Christ 'there is neither . . . male nor female'.[23] We are absolutely equal in worth, dignity and relation to God. The second affirmation is that the sexes are complementary. This is taught in Genesis 2:18–24. Equality does not mean identity. Nor does it necessarily imply roles that are completely interchangeable. Moreover, within this complementarity Paul affirmed the principle of masculine 'headship'. He derived it from the facts of creation in Genesis 2, namely that woman was made after, out of and for man. Evidently he did not see any conflict between this and Galatians 3:28. I do not myself feel at liberty to disagree with the apostle Paul or to dismiss his teaching as rabbinic, cultural or mistaken. On the contrary, he roots it in creation, and what creation has established, no culture is able to destroy.

From the two affirmations I come to the two questions. First, what does 'headship' mean? I do not think we shall find our answer from the etymology of the Greek word *kephalē*, 'head', or from its use in secular Greek where it may sometimes mean 'source'. The meaning of a word in Scripture is determined less by its origin or its use elsewhere than by its use in the biblical context. Given this, Ephesians 5:21–32 comes to our aid, since there Paul uses 'head' to convey responsibility rather than authority. He argues that the husband's headship (and therefore perhaps masculine headship in general) is to be modelled both on Christ's headship of the church (which led him to give himself up for her) and on our relation to our own body (which leads us to nourish it and care for it). In both cases 'headship' means sacrifice and service. It is the headship of care, not control. Its purpose is not to inhibit, let alone to crush, but to facilitate. Husbands are to create conditions of love and security in which women are free to be, and to develop, themselves.

Second, how does 'headship' apply? Does it forbid ordination or other forms of ministry? In 1 Corinthians 11, Paul requires women to wear veils in public worship and refers to the veil as a symbol of authority, which in those days it was. It still is in some cultures, but not in the West. Wearing hats in church is a good example of bad transposition, for Western women's hats tend to symbolize liberation rather than submission!

What then about the requirement of silence? My own belief is that commentators have not sufficiently noticed that Paul draws a double contrast when he writes, 'A woman should learn in quietness and full submission. I do not permit a woman to teach or to assume authority over a man; she must be silent.'[24] The first contrast is between authority and submission. This seems to be permanent because creational. The second contrast is between teaching and silence. Is it possible that silence, like the veil, was a first-century cultural symbol of submission to masculine headship, which is not necessarily binding today? Certainly the situation has changed considerably. Women in many cultures today are just as educated as men. And the teaching office today, now that the New Testament canon has been finalized, is much less authoritative. So, then, supposing (I ask myself) a woman were to teach men under the authority of Scripture (not claiming an authority of her own), in a meek and humble spirit (not throwing her weight about), and as a member of a pastoral team of which a man were head – might those three conditions enable her to teach men without exercising an improper authority over them, and without infringing the principle of masculine headship? Would this be a legitimate example of cultural transposition?

My tentative answer to my own questions is, 'Yes, I think so.' I realize that this may seem to some nothing but an irrelevant theory, since in several denominations and in many parts of the world women's ordination is already a reality. But at least I hope it is clear what I have been trying to do. This is to identify and preserve the essence of God's revelation (in this case the creational relation of the sexes), while at the same time seeking to discern appropriate contemporary cultural symbols to express it.

I conclude this rather long chapter with two words of reassurance about the practice of cultural transposition.

First, cultural transposition is appropriate only where the biblical text contains two levels of discourse – first, doctrinal or ethical teaching, and, second, its cultural or social expression; first (for example) the command to love and serve one another, and second the foot-washing. Cultural transposition is impossible where there is only one level of discourse. So it cannot be used to justify the rejection of what Scripture teaches, forbids or commands.

Take as an example the attempt to justify homosexual partnerships by declaring the biblical prohibitions to be culturally conditioned. The argument developed by some liberal thinkers runs like this: 'We grant that some forms of homosexual behaviour were forbidden by Moses in the Old Testament and by Paul in the New. But they were referring to particular cultural practices. In Leviticus they referred to the ritual prostitution which was part of ancient Canaanite fertility religion, and in Paul's letters to promiscuous sexual behaviour, together with the corruption of the young. They were not referring to tender, loving, faithful relationships between two adult men or two adult women. Besides, Moses and Paul had a very limited understanding of human psychosexuality. We know much more than they did. So, then, because the biblical prohibitions were of culturally specific taboos, they are irrelevant to us, and they cannot be taken to forbid a committed homosexual partnership which is equivalent to a heterosexual marriage.'

But this is a specious argument, which needs to be firmly rejected. The reason for the biblical prohibitions of homosexual conduct was not cultural, but creational. They arose from the biblical definition of marriage, which was personally endorsed by Jesus Christ: 'For this reason a man will leave his father and mother and be united to his wife, and the two will become one flesh.'[25] In other words, the only kind of marriage or sexual partnership envisaged in Scripture is heterosexual monogamy, which is also the only God-given context for the 'one-flesh' experience. So what limits sexual intercourse to heterosexual marriage, and forbids it in all other relationships, is not culture, but creation. No attempt at cultural transposition would be legitimate here.

Second, cultural transposition is not the thin end of the liberal wedge. It is not a conveniently respectable way to dodge awkward passages of Scripture by declaring them to be culturally relative. It is not a sophisticated way of rejecting biblical authority. No. If we go in for total rejection, we certainly cannot obey God's Word. If instead we embrace a position of wooden literalism, our obedience becomes artificial and mechanical. Only if we transpose the teaching of Scripture into modern cultural dress does our obedience become contemporary. Not disobedience, but meaningful obedience, is the purpose of cultural transposition.

Reflection questions from Tim Chester

1 Think of a passage of Scripture you have recently read or heard preached on. What would 'distancing' yourself from the text to avoid premature application involve? What would then 'entering' the text in its original setting with empathy involve?

2 Which experiences have you had of seeing your culture afresh by viewing it from the perspective of another culture?

3 Stott suggests our culture has blinded many Western evangelical Christians to the challenge of global hunger and indiscriminate weaponry. Do you agree? What do you think might be our cultural blind spots?

4 What should we do to avoid misreading or misapplying the Bible because we read it from the perspective of our cultural assumptions?

5 Stott says there are three responses to those parts of the Bible in which the truth is expressed in culturally specific ways: (1) *total rejection*; (2) *wooden literalism*; and (3) the faithful way of *cultural transposition*. Can you think of examples of issues where some people have opted for either total rejection or wooden literalism?

6 Look at Deuteronomy 22:8, Romans 16:16, Galatians 5:2 and Colossians 3:22. In each case, what would total rejection, wooden literalism and cultural transposition involve?

4

Expounding the Word

This chapter is about preaching, and as I begin it, I am conscious of the need to make three preliminary points.

The first is a personal one. There is something fundamentally anomalous about one preacher presuming to preach to other preachers about preaching. For what do I know that you do not know? We have all preached, read and listened to sermons ad nauseam. I certainly claim no particular expertise. Often still in the pulpit I am seized with a communication frustration. Seldom if ever do I descend from the pulpit without feeling the need to confess my comparative failure and to pray for grace to do better next time. So I hope this puts us on the same level. We are all struggling in this privileged but problematic ministry.

My second point is social. It concerns the widespread disillusion with preaching. It is widely considered an anachronism, an obsolete medium of communication, a dead art form, 'a sacred relic, a dubious thing of withered skin and dry bones enclosed in a reliquary of fond remembrance, still encrusted with the jewels of past glory'.[1] Who wants to listen to sermons any more? People are drugged by television and the internet, hostile to authority, weary and wary of words. When the sermon begins, they quickly grow impatient, fidgety and bored. We cannot assume that people want to listen to us; we have to fight for their attention.

Third, and speaking pastorally, in spite of the acknowledged problems, we must persevere. For the health of the church depends on it. If it is true, as Jesus said, endorsing Deuteronomy, that human beings do 'not live on bread alone, but on every word that comes from the mouth of God',[2] it is equally true of churches. Churches live, grow and flourish by the Word of God; they wilt and wither without it. The pew cannot easily rise higher than the pulpit. Indeed, the pew is usually a reflection of the pulpit. This is the lesson of history. 'Is it not clear,' asked Dr Martyn Lloyd-Jones, 'that the decadent periods and eras in the history of the Church have always been those periods when preaching had declined?'[3] I am sure he was right. Indeed, we can see it illustrated in the world today. Although we rejoice in the statistics of church growth, we have to admit with shame that it is often growth without depth. There is superficiality everywhere. And I am convinced from observation that the low level of Christian living is due more than anything else to the low level of Christian preaching. Yes, it is the Holy Spirit who renews the church, but the Spirit's sword is the Word of God.[4] Nothing, it seems to me, is more important for the life and growth, health and depth of the contemporary church than a recovery of serious biblical preaching.

Let me develop the case for biblical preaching. I begin with a straightforward definition in twenty-four words: 'To preach is to open up the inspired text with such faithfulness and sensitivity that God's voice is heard and God's people obey him.'

This definition of preaching contains six implications – two convictions about the biblical text, two obligations in expounding it and two expectations as a result.

Two convictions

The first conviction about the biblical text is that it is an inspired text. 'To preach is to open up the inspired text.' A high view of the biblical text – the recognition that it is unlike any other text, unique in its origin, nature and authority – is indispensable to authentic preaching. Nothing undermines preaching more than scepticism about Scripture. Without developing a sustained defence of this statement, I hope I shall carry you with me in reference to three words that belong together in our doctrine of Scripture, namely 'revelation', 'inspiration' and 'providence'.

'Revelation' describes the initiative God took to unveil or disclose himself. It is a humbling word. It presupposes that in his infinite perfections, God is altogether beyond the reach of our finite minds. Our mind cannot penetrate his mind. We have no ability to read his thoughts. Indeed, his thoughts are as much higher than our thoughts as the heavens are higher than the earth.[5] As a result, we would know nothing about God if he had not chosen to make himself known. Without revelation we would not be Christians at all, but Athenians, and all the world's altars would be inscribed 'TO AN UNKNOWN GOD'.[6] But we believe God has revealed himself, not only in the glory and order of the created universe, but supremely in Jesus Christ his incarnate Word, and in the written Word which bears a comprehensive and variegated witness to him.

'Inspiration' describes the means God chose by which to reveal himself, namely by speaking to and through the biblical authors. As we have already noted, it was not a dictation process that would have demeaned them into machines, but a dynamic one which treated them as persons in active possession of their faculties. Many of the biblical authors were historians, and much of Scripture is history. For this they engaged in research, and made use of diaries, records and archives. They were also theologians, each with a distinct doctrinal emphasis, and writers, each with his own literary genre, style and vocabulary. These phenomena of historical research, theological concern and literary composition were neither incompatible with, nor smothered by, the process of inspiration. God spoke through them in such a way that the words spoken were simultaneously and equally his and theirs. This is the double authorship of Scripture, on which we reflected in chapter 1.

The third word is 'providence'. This is the loving foresight and provision of God by which he arranged for the words he had spoken

- to be written so that they formed what we call 'Scripture';
- to be preserved across the centuries so as to be available to all people in all places at all times, for their salvation and enrichment.

Scripture, then, is 'God's word written',[7] his self-disclosure in speech and writing, the product of his revelation, inspiration and providence. This first conviction is indispensable to preachers. If God had not spoken, we would not dare to speak, for we would have nothing to say except our own threadbare speculations. But since God has spoken, we too must speak, communicating to others what he has communicated in Scripture. Indeed, we refuse to be silenced! As Amos put it, 'The Sovereign LORD has spoken – who can but prophesy?',[8] or pass on his Word. Similarly, Paul wrote, quoting Psalm 116, 'I believed; therefore I have spoken.'[9] In other words, we speak because we believe what God has spoken.

I pity the preacher who enters the pulpit with no Bible in his hands, or with a Bible that is more rags and tatters than the Word of God. He cannot expound Scripture, because he has no Scripture to expound. He cannot speak, for he has nothing worth saying. But to enter the pulpit with the confidence that God has spoken, that he has caused what he has spoken to be written, and that we have this inspired text in our hands – ah! then our head begins to swim, our heart to beat, our blood to flow and our eyes to sparkle, with the sheer glory of having God's Word in our hands and on our lips.

Our second conviction is that the inspired text is also a partially closed text. If to preach is 'to open up the inspired text', then it must be partially closed or it would not need to be opened up. And at once I think I see your Protestant hackles rising with indignation. 'What do you mean,' you ask me, 'that Scripture is partially closed? Do you not believe with the sixteenth-century Reformers in the "perspicuity" of Scripture (that it has a transparent or "see-through" quality)? Cannot even simple and uneducated people understand it by themselves? Is not the Holy Spirit our God-given teacher?' Yes, indeed;

thank you for your questions. I can say a resounding 'Yes' to them. But what you are rightly saying also needs to be qualified.

The Reformers' insistence on the perspicuity of Scripture related to its central message, namely the gospel of salvation through faith in Christ crucified. That is as plain as day in the Bible. But they did not maintain that everything in Scripture is equally plain. How could they when Peter wrote that some things in Paul's letters 'are hard to understand'?[10] If one apostle did not always understand another apostle, it would hardly be modest for us to claim that we see no problems! As a result, the church needs 'pastors and teachers' to expound or open up the Scriptures, and the ascended Christ still gives these gifts to his church.[11]

The story of the Ethiopian eunuch illustrates this need for human teachers. While he was sitting in his chariot and reading Isaiah 53, Philip asked him, 'Do you understand what you are reading?' Did the Ethiopian reply, 'Why, of course I do. Don't you believe in the perspicuity of Scripture?'? No, he said, 'How can I [understand] unless someone explains it to me?'[12] John Calvin rightly comments on the Ethiopian's humility, and contrasts it with those who, 'swollen-headed' with confidence in their own abilities, are too proud to submit themselves to teaching.

Here then is the biblical case for biblical exposition. It consists of two fundamental convictions, namely that God has given us in Scripture a text which is both inspired (having a divine origin and authority) and to some degree closed (difficult to understand). Therefore, in addition to the text, he gives the church teachers to open up the text, explaining it and applying it to people's lives.

Two obligations

My definition of preaching now moves on from two convictions about the biblical text to two obligations in expounding it. 'To preach is to open up the inspired text with . . . faithfulness and sensitivity . . .'

The main reason why the biblical text is partially closed and hard to understand is that a wide and deep cultural gulf yawns between the ancient world in which God spoke his Word and the modern world in which we listen to it. It is this cultural chasm, which occupied us in the last chapter, which also determines the task of the biblical expositor and lays down our two major obligations, namely faithfulness to the ancient Word and sensitivity to the modern world.

First comes the call to faithfulness. We have to accept the discipline of exegesis. We need to think ourselves back into the situation of the biblical authors, into their history, geography, culture and language. This task has long been graced with the name 'grammatico-historical exegesis'. To neglect this discipline, or to do it in a half-hearted or slovenly way, is inexcusable. That would express contempt for the way God chose to speak. With what painstaking, conscientious and meticulous care should we ourselves study, and open to others, the very words of the living God!

Moreover, the worst blunder that we can commit is to read back our twenty-first-century thoughts into the minds of the biblical authors (which is 'eisegesis'), to manipulate what they wrote in order to make it conform to what we want them to say, and then to claim their patronage for our opinions.

John Calvin, centuries in advance of his time, understood this principle well. 'It is the first business of an interpreter,' he wrote, 'to let his author say what he does say, instead of attributing to him what we think he ought to say.'[13] Some 300 years later, Charles Simeon of Cambridge set out the same principle in a letter to his publisher: 'My endeavour is to bring out of Scripture what is there, and not to thrust in what I think might be there.'[14] In our day we urgently need both the integrity and the courage to work by this basic rule, to give the biblical authors the freedom to say what they do say, however unfashionable and unpopular their teaching may be.

Second, biblical preaching demands sensitivity to the modern world. Although God spoke to the ancient world in its own languages and cultures, he intends his Word to be for everybody. This means that the expositor is more than an exegete. The exegete explains the original meaning of the text; the expositor goes further and applies it to the contemporary world. We have then to struggle to understand the rapidly changing world in which God has called us to live. We must grasp the main movements of thought which have shaped it. We must listen to its many discordant voices, its questions, its protests and its cries of pain. We must feel a measure of its disorientation and despair. For all this is part of our Christian sensitivity.

Here then are the two obligations which the call to preach lays upon biblical expositors – faithfulness (to the Word) and sensitivity (to the world). We are neither to falsify the Word to secure a phony relevance, nor to ignore the world to secure a phony faithfulness. We are not to fulfil either obligation at the expense of the other. It is the combination of faithfulness and sensitivity which makes the authentic preacher. And because it is difficult, it is also rare. The characteristic fault of conservative preachers is to be biblical, but not contemporary. The characteristic fault of liberal preachers is to be contemporary, but not biblical. Very few preachers manage to be both simultaneously.

In practice, as we study the text, we need to ask ourselves two distinct questions, and to ask them in the right order. The first is, 'What did it mean?' and the second, 'What does it say?' In posing these two questions, our concern begins with the text's original meaning, when it was first spoken or written, and then moves on to its contemporary message, as it addresses people today. We must neither confuse these two questions, nor put them in the wrong order, nor ask either without also asking the other.

The first question, 'What did it mean?', could also be worded 'What *does* it mean?', since a text's actual meaning does not change. It still means today what it meant when it was first written. In his well-known book *Validity in Interpretation*, Dr E. D. Hirsch, formerly

Kenan Professor of English at the University of Virginia, reaffirms the 'sensible belief that a text means what its author meant'.[15] He complains of the 'banishment of the author' from legal, biblical and literary texts. The result is pure subjectivism. As a result, in legal circles, 'the meaning of a law is what present judges say the meaning is'; in Bultmannian biblical exegesis, 'the meaning of the Bible is a new revelation to each succeeding generation'; and in literary theory, a text is 'what it means to us today'.[16] Indeed, in some university literature departments it is now claimed that 'a text is infinitely interpretable', because it 'means' different things to different people. But this is a misleading use of the words 'mean' and 'meaning'. Professor Hirsch insists that it is only the author who determines the meaning of a text, and that to 'banish the original author as the determiner of meaning' is to 'reject the only compelling normative principle that could lend validity to an interpretation'.[17] So a text's 'meaning' is what its author meant by it, and is therefore permanent, whereas its 'significance' is how it strikes different people and relates to different contexts, and is therefore variable.[18] There is all the difference in the world between Bultmann's 'a text means what it means to me' and E. D. Hirsch's 'a text means what its author meant'.

So the meaning of a text must be sought and found in the words themselves, the author's words, and not in the reader's thoughts and feelings. As Professor David Wells has put it, 'Meaning is not to be found above the text, behind it, beyond it, or in the interpreter. Meaning is to be found *in the text*. It is the language of the text which determines what meaning God intends for us to have.' This is because 'words have meanings ... No language allows meaning to float free of the words used ... Unless words and their meaning are re-joined in hermeneutical practice, we can have no access to revelation in anything but a mystical sense.'[19]

The second question we have to ask of the text is, 'What does it say?' That is, having discerned its original meaning (which is fixed by its author), we need next to reflect on its contemporary message (how it applies to people today). This is where spiritual sensitivity comes in. We have to increase our familiarity with the modern world – its presuppositions and preoccupations, its mentality and mood, its volatile culture and falling standards, its values, goals, doubts, fears, pains and hopes, and not least its obsession with self, love and death. Only then shall we be able to discern how the unchanging Word speaks to the changing world. Nothing has helped me to do this more than the reading group of younger professionals who have been meeting with me in London roughly every six weeks for the last twenty years. We agree at the end of each session which book to read or film to see before our next meeting. We choose mainly books and films that express a non-Christian perspective. Then we ask ourselves two questions:

1 What are the main issues which this raises for Christians?
2 How does the gospel relate to people who think and live like this?

In other words, we put our second question, 'What does it say?', to the biblical text.

If we grasp the original meaning of a text, without going on to grapple with its contemporary message, we surrender to antiquarianism, unrelated to the present realities of the modern world. If, on the other hand, we begin with the text's contemporary message, without first accepting the discipline of discovering its original meaning, we surrender to existentialism, unrelated to the past realities of revelation. Instead, we must ask both questions, first being faithful in working at the text's meaning and then being sensitive in discerning its message for today. Moreover, there are no short cuts to this. There is only the hard slog of study, seeking to become familiar both with the Scriptures in their fullness and with the modern world in all its variety.

It is, in fact, another case of the discipline of 'double listening', as we listen humbly to Scripture and critically to modernity, in order to relate the one to the other. Such listening is an indispensable preliminary to preaching.

The Archbishop of Canterbury's Special Envoy Terry Waite successfully negotiated the release of several hostages in the Middle East. Eventually he himself was taken captive by a Lebanese group known as Islamic Jihad, and held for five years. On 18 November 1991, the day he was finally released, one of the hostages whose liberation he had negotiated was asked for a comment. Jean Waddell, a former missionary in Iran, replied, 'He's such a good communicator; he listens.'

Two expectations

After the two convictions about Scripture, and the two obligations in expounding it, come two resulting expectations. If we do open up the inspired text with faithfulness and sensitivity, what can we expect to happen?

First, we expect God's voice to be heard. This expectation arises from our belief that the God who has spoken in the past also speaks in the present through what he has spoken.

Such an expectation, that through his ancient Word God addresses the modern world, is, however, at a low ebb today. As Dr Langmead Casserley, a scholar of the American Episcopal Church, has said, 'We have devised a way of reading the Word of God, from which no word from God ever comes.' When the time for the sermon arrives, the people clasp their hands and close their eyes with a fine show of piety, and sit back for their customary doze. And the preacher encourages this by his soporific voice and manner.

How different it is when both preacher and people are expecting God to speak! The whole situation is transformed and becomes electric. The people bring their Bibles to church, and when they open them, they sit on the edge of their seats, hungrily waiting for what the Lord God may have to say to them. It is a re-enactment of the scene in the house of Cornelius the centurion when the apostle Peter arrived. Cornelius said to him, 'Now we are all here in the presence of God to listen to everything the Lord has commanded you to tell us.'[20] Why may a Christian congregation not experience the same degree of expectation today?

The preacher himself can encourage this attitude. He prepares carefully, in such a way that he is evidently expecting God to give him a message. He prays earnestly before he leaves home, and prays again in the pulpit before he preaches, that God will speak to his people. He reads and expounds his text with great seriousness of purpose, feeling deeply what he is talking about. Then, when he has finished and he prays again, there is a stillness and a solemnity in the presence of the God who has spoken.

Our second expectation is that God's people will obey him. The Word of God always demands a response of obedience. We are not to be forgetful hearers, but obedient doers, of God's Word.[21] Throughout the Old Testament we hear the divine lament, 'Today, oh that you would listen to my voice!'[22] God kept sending his envoys to his people, 'But they mocked God's messengers, despised his words and scoffed at his prophets until the wrath of the LORD was aroused against his people and there was no remedy.'[23]

How then should people respond? What kind of obedience is required? Our answer is that the nature of the response expected is determined by the content of the word expounded. What we *do* in response to God's Word depends on what he *says* to us through it. Consider some examples. If, in and through the text expounded, God speaks about himself and his own glorious greatness, then we respond by humbling ourselves before him in worship. If instead he speaks about us, our waywardness, fickleness, rebellion and guilt, then we respond in penitence and confession. If he speaks about Jesus Christ, who died to bear our sins and was raised from the dead to prove it, we respond in faith, laying hold of this heaven-sent Saviour. If he speaks about his promises, we determine to inherit them; if about his commands, we determine to keep them. If God speaks to us about the world, and its colossal spiritual and material need, then his compassion rises within us both to preach the gospel and to serve the needy. If, on the other hand, God speaks to us through his Word about the future coming of Christ and the glory to follow, then our hope is kindled, and we resolve to be holy and busy until he comes.

The preacher who has penetrated deeply into his text, who has isolated and unfolded its dominant theme, and has himself been moved by its message, will hammer it home in his conclusion, and give people a chance to respond to it, often in silent prayer, as each person is brought by the Holy Spirit to an appropriate obedience.

This, then, is the definition of preaching which I offer you. It contains two convictions (that the biblical text is an inspired text which nevertheless needs to be opened up), two obligations (that we must open it up with faithfulness to the text itself and sensitivity to the modern context) and two expectations (that through the exposition and application of the written Word, God himself will speak, and that his people will hear his voice and respond to him in obedience).

It is an enormous privilege to be a biblical expositor – to stand in the pulpit with God's Word in our hands and minds, God's Spirit in our hearts and God's people before our eyes, waiting expectantly for God's voice to be heard and obeyed.

Reflection questions from Tim Chester

1 What makes preaching (and listening to preaching) hard in our day? What makes it vital?
2 How would you define preaching? How does your definition correspond to, or differ from, the definition given by Stott?

3 What happens if we do not share Stott's two convictions: (1) that Scripture is both inspired (having a divine origin and authority) and (2) that Scripture is to some degree closed (difficult to understand)? Have you seen this happening?

4 Stott says we must ask of the text of Scripture 'What did it mean?' and 'What does it say?', in that order. What happens if we ask one question without the other? What happens if we ask them in the wrong order? Can you think of examples of these faults?

5 In which ways are you engaged in the 'double listening' to which Stott calls us? What else could you do?

6 Stott says we should expect God's voice to be heard when his Word is preached. How can we foster this expectation in our own hearts? In the life of our church?

Conclusion
The now and the not yet

I began in the Introduction with the tension between the 'then' (past) and the 'now' (present); I end with another tension, between the 'now' (present) and the 'not yet' (future). These two tensions belong together. For it is in and through Jesus Christ that the past, the present and the future are brought into a creative relationship. Christians live in the present, but do so in thankfulness for the past and in anticipation of the future.

As I conclude this book, I'm going to focus on balanced biblical Christianity. Balance is a rare commodity these days in almost every sphere, not least among us who seek to follow Christ.

One of the things about the devil is that he is a fanatic, and the enemy of all common sense, moderation and balance. One of his favourite pastimes is to tip Christians off balance. If he cannot get us to *deny* Christ, he will get us to *distort* Christ instead. As a result, lopsided Christianity is widespread, in which we overemphasize one aspect of a truth, while underemphasizing another.

A balanced grasp of the now–not-yet tension would be very beneficial for Christian unity, and especially to a greater harmony among evangelical believers. We may agree on the doctrinal and ethical fundamentals of the faith. Yet we seem to be constitutionally prone to quarrelling and dividing, or simply to going our own way and building our own empires.

Kingdom come and coming

Fundamental to New Testament Christianity is the perspective that we are living 'in between times' – between the first and the second comings of Christ, between kingdom come and kingdom coming.

The theological basis for this tension is to be found in Jesus' own teaching about the kingdom of God. Everyone accepts both that the kingdom featured prominently in his teaching and that he announced its coming. Where scholars have disagreed, however, is over the time of its arrival. Has the kingdom already come, because Jesus brought it with him? Or is its coming still in the future, so that we await it expectantly? Or does the truth lie between these positions?

Albert Schweitzer is an example of a scholar who thought that, according to Jesus, the kingdom lay entirely in the future. As an apocalyptic prophet, Jesus taught (mistakenly) that God was about to intervene supernaturally and establish his kingdom. The radical demands he made on his disciples were an 'interim ethic' in the light of the imminent arrival of the kingdom. Schweitzer's position is known as 'thoroughgoing' or 'consistent' eschatology.

At the opposite extreme was C. H. Dodd, with his belief that the coming of the kingdom is wholly in the past (known as 'realized eschatology'). He laid a heavy emphasis on two verses whose verbs are in the perfect tense, namely 'The kingdom of God has arrived'[1] and 'The kingdom of God has come upon you.'[2] Dodd concluded that there is no future coming of the kingdom, and that passages which speak of one were not part of Jesus' own teaching.

In place of these extreme polarities, most scholars have taken a middle position – that Jesus spoke of the kingdom as both a present reality and a future expectation.

Jesus clearly taught that the time of fulfilment had arrived;[3] that 'the strong man' was now bound and disarmed, enabling the plundering of his goods, as was evident from his exorcisms;[4] that the kingdom was already either 'within' or 'among' people,[5] and that it could now be 'entered' or 'received'.[6]

Yet the kingdom was a future expectation as well. It would not be perfected until the last day. So he looked forward to the end, and taught his disciples to do so also. They were to pray 'your kingdom come'[7] and to 'seek' it first,[8] giving priority to its expansion. At times he also referred to the final state of his followers in terms of 'entering' the kingdom[9] or 'receiving' it.[10]

One way in which the Bible expresses the tension between the 'now' and the 'not yet' is in the terminology of the two 'ages'. From the perspective of the Old Testament, history is divided between 'this present age' and 'the last days', namely the kingdom of righteousness to be introduced by the Messiah.[11] This simple structure of two consecutive ages was decisively changed, however, by the coming of Jesus. For he brought in the new age, and died for us in order to deliver us 'from the present evil age'.[12] As a result, the Father has already 'rescued us from the dominion of darkness and brought us into the kingdom of the Son he loves'.[13] We have even been raised from death and seated with Christ in the heavenly realm.[14]

At the same time, the old age persists. So the two ages overlap. 'The darkness is passing and the true light is already shining.' One day the old age will be terminated (which will be 'the end of the age'),[15] and the new age, which was introduced with Christ's first coming, will be brought about at his second. Meanwhile, the two ages continue, and we are caught in the tension between them. We are summoned not to 'conform to the pattern of this world', but rather to 'be transformed' according to God's will and to live consistently as children of the light.[16]

Nevertheless, the tension remains: we have already *been* saved, yet also we *shall* be saved one day.[17] And we are already God's adopted children, yet we also are waiting for our adoption.[18] Already we have 'crossed over from death to life', yet eternal life is also a future gift.[19] Already Christ is reigning, although his enemies have not yet become his footstool.[20]

Caught between the present and the future, the characteristic stance of Christians is variously described as hoping,[21] waiting,[22] longing,[23] and groaning,[24] as we wait both 'eagerly'[25] and also 'patiently'.[26]

The essence of the interim period between the 'now' and the 'not yet' is the presence of the Holy Spirit in the people of God. On the one hand, the gift of the Spirit is the distinctive blessing of the kingdom of God and the principal sign that the new age has dawned.[27] On the other, because his indwelling is only the beginning of our kingdom inheritance, it is also the guarantee that the rest will one day be ours. The New Testament uses three metaphors to illustrate this. The Holy Spirit is the 'firstfruits', pledging that the full harvest will follow,[28] the 'deposit' or first instalment, pledging that the full payment will be made,[29] and the foretaste, pledging that the full feast will one day be enjoyed.[30]

Here are some examples of the tension between the 'now' and the 'not yet'.

Revelation, holiness and healing

The first example is in *the intellectual sphere*, or the question of *revelation*.

We affirm with joyful confidence that God has revealed himself to human beings, not only in the created universe, in our reason and our conscience, but supremely in his Son Jesus Christ, and in the Bible's witness to him, as we saw earlier. We dare to say that we know God, because he has himself taken the initiative to draw aside the curtain which would otherwise hide him from us. We rejoice greatly that his Word throws light on our path.[31]

But we do not yet know God as he knows us. Our knowledge is partial because his revelation has been partial. He has revealed everything which he intends to reveal, and which he considers to be for our good, but not everything that there is to reveal. There are many mysteries left, and so 'we live by faith, not by sight'.[32]

We should take our stand alongside those biblical authors who, although they knew themselves to be agents of divine revelation, nevertheless confessed humbly that their knowledge remained limited. Even Moses, 'whom the LORD knew face to face', acknowledged, 'O Sovereign LORD, you have only [RSV] begun to show to your servant your greatness and your strong hand.'[33] Then think of the apostle Paul, who likened his knowledge both to the immature thoughts of a child and to the distorted reflections of a mirror.[34]

So, then, although it is right to glory in the givenness and finality of God's revelation, it is also right to confess our ignorance of many things. We know and we don't know. 'The secret things belong to the LORD our God, but the things revealed belong to us and to our children for ever, that we may follow all the words of this law.'[35] It is very important to maintain this distinction. Speaking personally, I would like to see more boldness in our proclaiming what has been revealed, and more reticence about what has been kept secret. Agreement in plainly revealed truth is necessary for unity, even while we give each other freedom in secondary matters. And the way to recognize these is when Christians who are equally anxious to be submissive to Scripture nevertheless reach different conclusions about them. I am thinking, for example, about controversies over baptism, church government, liturgy and ceremonies, claims about spiritual gifts, and the fulfilment of prophecy.

The second tension is in *the moral sphere*, or the question of *holiness*.

God has already put his Holy Spirit within us, in order to make us holy.[36] The Holy Spirit is actively at work within us, subduing our fallen, selfish human nature and causing his fruit to ripen in our character.[37] Already, we can affirm, he is transforming us into the image of Christ.[38]

But our fallen nature has not been eradicated, for 'the flesh desires what is contrary to the Spirit',[39] so that 'if we claim to be without sin, we deceive ourselves'.[40] We have not yet become completely conformed to God's perfect will, for we do not yet love God with all our being, or our neighbour as ourselves. As Paul put it, we have 'not . . . already become perfect' (GNT), but we 'press on towards the goal', confident that 'he who began a good work in [us] will carry it on to completion until the day of Christ Jesus'.[41]

So, then, we are caught in a painful tension between the 'now' and the 'not yet', between dismay over our continuing failures and the promise of ultimate freedom. On the one hand, we must take God's command, 'Be holy because I . . . am holy',[42] and Jesus' instruction, 'Go, and do not sin again',[43] with the utmost seriousness. On the other hand, we have to acknowledge the reality of indwelling sin alongside the reality of the indwelling Spirit.[44] The sinless perfection we long for continues to elude us.

The third tension between the 'already' and the 'not yet' is to be found in *the physical sphere* or the question of *healing*.

We affirm that the long-promised kingdom of God broke into history with Jesus Christ, who was not content merely to *proclaim* the kingdom, but went on to *demonstrate* its arrival by the extraordinary things he did. His power was especially evident in the human body as he healed the sick, expelled demons and raised the dead.

He also gave authority to both the Twelve and the Seventy to extend his mission in Israel, and to perform miracles. How much wider he intended his authority to go is a matter of dispute. Generally speaking, miracles were 'the signs of a true apostle'.[45] Nevertheless, it would be foolish to attempt to limit or domesticate God. We must allow him his freedom and his sovereignty, and be entirely open to the possibility of physical miracles today.

But God's kingdom has not yet come in its fullness. For 'the kingdom of the world' has not yet 'become the kingdom of our Lord and of his Christ' when 'he will reign for ever and ever'.[46] In particular, our bodies have not yet been redeemed, and nature has not yet been entirely brought under Christ's rule.

So we have to recognize the 'already'–'not-yet' tension in this sphere too. To be sure, we have 'tasted . . . the powers of the coming age',[47] but so far it has been only a taste. Part of our Christian experience is that the resurrection life of Jesus is 'revealed in our mortal body'.[48] At the same time, our bodies remain frail and mortal. To claim perfect health now would be to anticipate our resurrection. The bodily resurrection of Jesus was the pledge, and indeed the beginning, of God's new creation. But God has not yet uttered the decisive word, 'I am making everything new!'[49] Those who dismiss the very possibility of miracles today forget the 'already' of the kingdom, while those who expect them as what has been called 'the normal Christian life' forget that the kingdom is 'not yet'.

Church and society

Fourth, the same tension is experienced in *the ecclesiastical sphere*, or the question of *church discipline*.

Jesus the Messiah is gathering round him a people of his own, a community characterized by the truth, love and holiness to which he has called it. But Christ has not yet presented his bride to himself 'as a radiant church, without stain or wrinkle or any other blemish, but holy and blameless'.[50] On the contrary, her present life and witness are marred by error, discord and sin.

So, then, whenever we think about the church, we need to hold together the ideal and the reality. The church is both committed to truth and prone to error, both united and divided, both pure and impure. Not that we are to accept its failures. We are to cherish the vision of both the doctrinal and ethical purity and the visible unity of the church. We are called to 'fight the good fight of the faith',[51] and to 'make every effort to keep the unity of the Spirit through the bond of peace'.[52] And in pursuit of these things there is a place for discipline in cases of serious heresy or sin.

And yet error and evil are not going to be eradicated completely from the church in this world. They will continue to coexist with truth and goodness. 'Let both grow together until the harvest,' Jesus said in the parable of the wheat and the weeds.[53] Neither the Bible nor church history justifies the use of severe disciplinary measures in an attempt to secure a perfectly pure church in this world.

The fifth area of tension between the 'now' and the 'then', the 'already' and the 'not yet', is *the social sphere*, or the question of *progress*.

We affirm that God is at work in human society. This is partly in his 'common grace', as he gives the world the blessings of family and government, by which evil is restrained and relationships are ordered. And it is also through the members of his redeemed community, who penetrate society like salt and light, making a difference by hindering decay and dispelling darkness.

But God has not yet created the promised 'new heaven and . . . new earth, where righteousness dwells'.[54] There are still 'wars and rumours of wars'.[55] Swords have not yet been beaten into ploughshares and spears into pruning hooks.[56] The nations have not yet renounced war as a method of settling their disputes. Selfishness, cruelty and fear continue.

So, then, although it is right to campaign for social justice and to expect to improve society further, we know that we shall never perfect it. Although we know the transforming power of the gospel and the wholesome effects of Christian salt and light, we also know that evil is ingrained in human nature and human society. Only Christ at his second coming will eradicate evil and enthrone righteousness for ever.

Here, then, are five areas (intellectual, moral, physical, ecclesiastical and social) in which it is vital to preserve the tension between the 'already' and the 'not yet'.

Three types of Christian

There are three distinct types of Christian, according to the extent to which they manage to maintain this biblical balance.

First, there are the *'already' Christians* who emphasize what God has already given us in Christ. But they give the impression that, in consequence, there are now no mysteries left, no sins that cannot be overcome, no diseases that cannot be healed, and no evils that cannot be eradicated. In short, they seem to believe that perfection is attainable now.

Their motives are blameless. They want to glorify Christ – so they refuse to set limits to what he is able to do. But their optimism can easily degenerate into presumption and end up in disillusion. They forget the 'not yet' of the New Testament, and that perfection awaits the second coming of Christ.

Second, there are *the 'not-yet' Christians* who emphasize the incompleteness for the time being of the work of Christ and look forward to the time when he will complete what he has begun. But they seem to be preoccupied with our human ignorance and failure, the pervasive reign of disease and death, and the impossibility of securing either a pure church or a perfect society.

Their motive is excellent too. If the 'already' Christians want to glorify Christ, the 'not-yet' Christians want to humble sinners. They are determined to be true to the Bible in their emphasis on our human depravity. But their pessimism can easily degenerate into complacency; it can also lead to acceptance of the status quo and to apathy in the face of evil. They forget the 'already' of what Christ has done by his death, resurrection and gift of the Spirit – and of what he can do in our lives, and in church and society, as a result.

Third, there are *the 'already–not-yet' Christians*. They want to give equal weight to the two comings of Jesus. On the one hand, they have great confidence in the 'already', in what God has said and done through Christ. On the other hand, they exhibit a genuine humility before the 'not yet', humility to confess that the world will remain fallen and half-saved until Christ perfects at his second coming what he began at his first.

It is this combination of the 'already' and the 'not yet' which characterizes authentic biblical evangelicalism, and which exemplifies the balance that is so urgently needed today.

Our position as 'contemporary Christians' rests securely on the person of Jesus, whose death and resurrection belong to the 'already' of the past, and whose glorious second coming to the 'not yet' of the future. As we acclaim in faith and triumph:

Christ has died!
Christ is risen!
Christ will come again!

Notes

Preface
1 Revelation 1:8.
2 Hebrews 13:8.

**Series introduction: the Contemporary Christian –
the then and the now**
1 Psalm 119:105; cf. 2 Peter 1:19.
2 Dietrich Bonhoeffer, *Letters and Papers from Prison*, enlarged edn
(SCM Press, 1971), p. 279.
3 Matthew 11:19.
4 See Jaroslav Pelikan, *Jesus Through the Centuries* (Yale University
Press, 1985), pp. 182–193.
5 2 Corinthians 11:4.
6 2 Timothy 1:15; cf. 4:11, 16.
7 Acts 26:25.
8 Ezekiel 2:6–7.

The Bible: introduction
1 Psalm 19:10

1 Continuing in the Word
1 2 Thessalonians 2:15.
2 Hebrews 2:1.
3 1 John 2:24.
4 2 John 9.
5 E.g. 1 Timothy 6:20; 2 Timothy 1:14.
6 Cf. Mark 1:15; 1 Corinthians 10:11.
7 E.g. Matthew 6:1–18.
8 C. S. Lewis, *Surprised by Joy* (Geoffrey Bles, 1955), p. 63.

9 Allan Bloom, *The Closing of the American Mind* (Simon & Schuster, 1987), p. 41.

10 Cf. John 5:39; 20:31.

11 J.-J. von Allmen, *Preaching and Congregation* (Lutterworth, 1962), p. 24.

12 E.g. Isaiah 1:20.

13 E.g. Acts 3:18, 21 (RSV).

14 Hebrews 1:1.

15 2 Peter 1:21.

16 J. I. Packer, *'Fundamentalism' and the Word of God* (IVP, 1958), pp. 81–82.

17 Cf. 2 Timothy 2:7.

18 Philemon 9.

19 Psalm 90:10 (AV).

2 Responding to the Word

1 Acts 17:23.

2 Mark 12:30.

3 John 4:24.

4 Psalm 105:3.

5 Luke 8:25; Mark 11:22.

6 John 14:15.

7 John 14:21.

8 Hebrews 10:23.

9 Mark 13:26; 14:62.

10 2 Peter 3:13.

11 Matthew 11:28–30.

12 2 Corinthians 10:5.

13 Luke 10:16.

14 John 17:20–23.

15 Ephesians 4:3.

16 *Op. Calv.* XIV, pp. 312–314, quoted in Jean Cadier, *The Man God Mastered* (ET IVF, 1960), pp. 172–173.

17 Ephesians 2:20.

18 E.g. Mark 7:5–13.

19 David H. C. Read, *Go and Make Disciples* (Abingdon, 1978), pp. 94–95.

3 Transposing the Word

1 Anthony C. Thiselton, *The Two Horizons: New Testament Hermeneutics and Philosophical Description with Special Reference to Heidegger, Bultmann, Gadamer and Wittgenstein* (Paternoster, 1980). Two shorter essays have brought this debate within reach of ordinary mortals, namely Dr Thiselton's own 'Understanding God's Word Today', in John Stott (ed.), *Obeying Christ in a Changing World*, Vol. I (Collins, 1977), pp. 90–122, and Dr J. I. Packer's 'Infallible Scripture and the Role of Hermeneutics', in D. A. Carson and John D. Woodbridge (eds.), *Scripture and Truth*, (Zondervan and IVP, 1983), pp. 323–356.

2 A. C. Thiselton, *The Two Horizons*, p. 103.

3 *Obeying Christ in a Changing World*, Vol. I, p. 118.

4 A. C. Thiselton, *The Two Horizons*, p. 326.

5 See e.g. *The Willowbank Report: Gospel and Culture* (Lausanne Committee for World Evangelization, 1978), pp. 10–11.

6 Psalm 119:18.

7 Isaiah 42:18–19.

8 Romans 12:2.

9 Jeffrey Sachs, *The End of Poverty* (Penguin, 2011).

10 From a book review in the *Church Times*.

11 See *The Willowbank Report: Gospel and Culture*, especially ch. 5.

12 See E. Stanley Jones, *The Christ of the Indian Road* (Hodder & Stoughton, 1926), e.g. p. 186.

13 Verse 3.

14 Verses 4, 5, 10.

15 Verse 8.

16 E.g. Psalm 74:14; Isaiah 27:1.

17 Psalm 19:1–6.

18 John 13:14.

19 Paul deals with this issue at some length in both Romans 14 and
    1 Corinthians 8.

20 1 Corinthians 8:4–6.

21 1 Timothy 2:12.

22 1 Corinthians 11:4–10; 14:34–35; 1 Timothy 2:11–12.

23 Galatians 3:28.

24 1 Timothy 2:11–12.

25 Genesis 2:24, quoted by Jesus in Mark 10:7–9, with the addition,
    'Therefore what God has joined together, let no one separate.'

4 Expounding the Word

1 George Target, *Words That Have Moved the World* (Bishopsgate,
   1987), p. 13.

2 Matthew 4:4; Deuteronomy 8:3.

3 D. Martyn Lloyd-Jones, *Preaching and Preachers* (Hodder &
   Stoughton, 1971), p. 24.

4 Ephesians 6:17.

5 Isaiah 55:9.

6 Acts 17:23.

7 Article XX of the Church of England's *Thirty-Nine Articles* (1563).

8 Amos 3:8.

9 2 Corinthians 4:13; Psalm 116:10.

10 2 Peter 3:16.

11 Ephesians 4:11.

12 Acts 8:26–39.

13 Quoted by F. W. Farrer in his *History of Interpretation*, the 1885
    Bampton Lectures (Macmillan, 1886), p. 347.

14 Quoted by Hugh Evan Hopkins in *Charles Simeon of Cambridge*
    (Hodder & Stoughton, 1977), p. 57.

15 E. D. Hirsch, *Validity in Interpretation* (Yale University Press,
    1967), p. 1.

16 Ibid., p. viii.

17 Ibid., p. 5.

18 Ibid., pp. 8, 255. Cf. also E. D. Hirsch, *The Aims of Interpretation* (University of Chicago Press, 1976), pp. 2–3, 79.

19 From Dr David Wells' essay, 'Word and World', in Kenneth S. Kantzer and Carl F. H. Henry (eds.), *Evangelical Affirmations* (Zondervan, 1990), pp. 161–162.

20 Acts 10:33.

21 James 1:22–25.

22 E.g. Psalm 95:7–10.

23 2 Chronicles 36:16.

Conclusion: the now and the not yet

1 Mark 1:15, as he translates *ēngiken*.

2 Matthew 12:28, *ephthasen*.

3 E.g. Matthew 13:16–17; Mark 1:14.

4 Matthew 12:28–29; cf. Luke 10:17–18.

5 Luke 17:20–21.

6 E.g. Mark 10:15.

7 Matthew 6:10.

8 Matthew 6:33.

9 Mark 9:47; cf. Matthew 8:11.

10 Matthew 25:34.

11 E.g. Isaiah 2:2; Matthew 12:32; Mark 10:30.

12 Galatians 1:4.

13 Colossians 1:13; cf. Acts 26:18; 1 Peter 2:9.

14 Ephesians 2:6; Colossians 3:1.

15 E.g. Matthew 13:39; 28:20.

16 Romans 12:2; 13:11–14; 1 Thessalonians 5:4–8.

17 Romans 8:24; 5:9–10; 13:11.

18 Romans 8:15, 23.

19 John 5:24; 11:25–26; Romans 8:10–11.

20 Psalm 110:1; Ephesians 1:22; Hebrews 2:8.

21 Romans 8:24.
22 Philippians 3:20–21; 1 Thessalonians 1:9–10.
23 Romans 8:19.
24 Romans 8:22–23, 26; 2 Corinthians 5:2, 4.
25 Romans 8:23; 1 Corinthians 1:7.
26 Romans 8:25.
27 E.g. Isaiah 32:15; 44:3; Ezekiel 39:29; Joel 2:28; Mark 1:8; Hebrews 6:4–5.
28 Romans 8:23.
29 2 Corinthians 5:5; Ephesians 1:14.
30 Hebrews 6:4–5.
31 Psalm 119:105.
32 2 Corinthians 5:7.
33 Deuteronomy 34:10; cf. Numbers 12:8; Deuteronomy 3:24.
34 1 Corinthians 13:9–12.
35 Deuteronomy 29:29.
36 1 Thessalonians 4:7–8.
37 Galatians 5:16–26.
38 2 Corinthians 3:18.
39 Galatians 5:17.
40 1 John 1:8.
41 Philippians 3:12–14; 1:6.
42 E.g. Leviticus 19:2.
43 John 8:11 (RSV).
44 E.g. Romans 7:17, 20; 8:9, 11.
45 2 Corinthians 12:12 (RSV).
46 Revelation 11:15.
47 Hebrews 6:5.
48 2 Corinthians 4:10–11.
49 Revelation 21:5.
50 Ephesians 5:27; cf. Revelation 21:2.
51 1 Timothy 6:12.
52 Ephesians 4:3.

53 Matthew 13:30.
54 2 Peter 3:13; Revelation 21:1.
55 Mark 13:7.
56 Isaiah 2:4.

Enjoyed this book? Read the rest of the series.

With the God's Word for Today series, John Stott's classic book *The Contemporary Christian* is now available in five individual parts for today's audiences. The text has been sensitively modernized and updated by Tim Chester but retains the original core, clear and crucial Bible teaching.

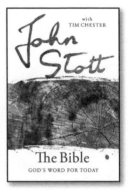

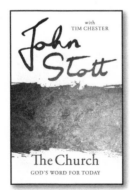

Find all five volumes at ivpress.com/god-s-word-for-today.

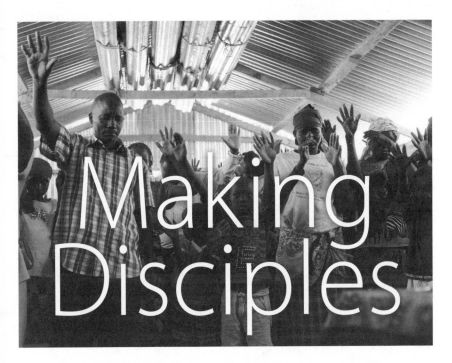

Making Disciples

Around the World — Christianity is exploding with growth in numbers

Yet — Believers are struggling to grow in Christ

That's Why Langham Exists

Our Vision

To see churches in the Majority World equipped for mission and growing to maturity in Christ through the ministry of pastors and leaders who believe, teach and live by the Word of God.

www.langham.org

FOUNDED BY JOHN STOTT